DATE DUE	
JAN I 9 1988	
FEB - 9 1988	
JUN 3 1991	
FEB 2 0 1993	
MAR 7 1994	
BRODART, INC	Cat. No. 23-221

SIMÓN BOLÍVAR

SIMÓN BOLÍVAR

Dennis Wepman

1985
CHELSEA HOUSE PUBLISHERS
NEW YORK

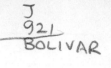

MANAGING EDITOR: William P. Hansen
ASSOCIATE EDITOR: John Haney
EDITORIAL COORDINATOR: Karyn Gullen Browne
EDITORIAL STAFF: Richard Mandell
　　　　　　　Jennifer Caldwell
　　　　　　　Paula Edelson
ART DIRECTOR: Susan Lusk
ART ASSISTANTS: Carol McDougall, Teresa Clark
LAYOUT: Irene Friedman
COVER DESIGN: Peterson Design
PICTURE RESEARCH: Keith Triller, John Haney

First Printing

Library of Congress Cataloging in Publication Data
Wepman, Dennis.
　　Simón Bolívar.
　　(World leaders past & present)
　　Bibliography: p.
　　Includes index.
　　1. Bolívar, Simón, 1783–1830. 2. Heads of state—
South America—Biography. I. Title. II. Series.
F2235.3.W46　1985　　980'.02'0924 [B]　　84-27499
ISBN 0-87754-569-3

Chelsea House Publishers
Harold Steinberg, Chairman & Publisher
Susan Lusk, Vice President
A Division of Chelsea House Educational Communications, Inc.

Chelsea House Publishers
133 Christopher Street
New York 10014

Photos courtesy of the Bettmann Archive and the New York Public Library

Contents

On Leadership, Arthur M. Schlesinger, jr. 7
1. The Playboy (1783–1799) 13
2. The Idealist (1799–1805) 27
3. The Firebrand (1805–1811) 41
4. The Soldier (1811–1812) 59
5. The Liberator (1812–1824) 69
6. The Exile (1824–1830) 101
Chronology . . . . : . 107
Further Reading 108
Index 109

C H E L S E A   H O U S E   P U B L I S H E R S

W O R L D   L E A D E R S   P A S T   &   P R E S E N T

ADENAUER
ALEXANDER THE GREAT
MARK ANTONY
KING ARTHUR
KEMAL ATATÛRK
CLEMENT ATTLEE
BEGIN
BEN GURION
BISMARCK
LEON BLUM
BOLÍVAR
CESARE BORGIA
BRANDT
BREZHNEV
CAESAR
CALVIN
CASTRO
CATHERINE THE GREAT
CHARLEMAGNE
CHIANG KAI-SHEK
CHOU EN-LAI
CHURCHILL
CLEMENCEAU
CLEOPATRA
CORTEZ
CROMWELL
DANTON
DE GAULLE
DE VALERA
DISRAELI
EISENHOWER
ELEANOR OF AQUITAINE
QUEEN ELIZABETH I
FERDINAND AND ISABELLA

FRANCO
FREDERICK THE GREAT
INDIRA GANDHI
GANDHI
GARIBALDI
GENGHIS KHAN
GLADSTONE
HAMMARSKJÖLD
HENRY VIII
HENRY OF NAVARRE
HINDENBURG
HITLER
HO CHI MINH
KING HUSSEIN
IVAN THE TERRIBLE
ANDREW JACKSON
JEFFERSON
JOAN OF ARC
POPE JOHN XXIII
LYNDON JOHNSON
BENITO JUÁREZ
JFK
KENYATTA
KHOMEINI
KHRUSHCHEV
MARTIN LUTHER KING
KISSINGER
LENIN
LINCOLN
LLOYD GEORGE
LOUIS XIV
LUTHER
JUDAS MACCABEUS

MAO
MARY, QUEEN OF SCOTS
GOLDA MEIR
METTERNICH
MUSSOLINI
NAPOLEON
NASSER
NEHRU
NERO
NICHOLAS II
NIXON
NKRUMAH
PERICLES
PERÓN
QADDAFI
ROBESPIERRE
ELEANOR ROOSEVELT
FDR
THEODORE ROOSEVELT
SADAT
SUN YAT-SEN
STALIN
TAMERLAINE
THATCHER
TITO
TROTSKY
TRUDEAU
TRUMAN
QUEEN VICTORIA
WASHINGTON
CHAIM WEIZMANN
WOODROW WILSON
XERXES

Further titles in preparation

ON LEADERSHIP

Arthur M. Schlesinger, jr.

LEADERSHIP, it may be said, is really what makes the world go round. Love no doubt smooths the passage; but love is a private transaction between consenting adults. Leadership is a public transaction with history. The idea of leadership affirms the capacity of individuals to move, inspire and mobilize masses of people so that they act together in pursuit of an end. Sometimes leadership serves good purposes, sometimes bad; but whether the end is benign or evil, great leaders are those men and women who leave their personal stamp on history.

Now, the very concept of leadership implies the proposition that individuals can make a difference. This proposition has never been universally accepted. From classical times to the present day, eminent thinkers have regarded individuals as no more than the agents and pawns of larger forces, whether the gods and goddesses of the ancient world or, in the modern era, race, class, nation, the dialectic, the will of the people, the spirit of the times, history itself. Against such forces, the individual dwindles into insignificance.

So contends the thesis of historical determinism. Tolstoy's great novel *War and Peace* offers a famous statement of the case. Why, Tolstoy asked, did millions of men in the Napoleonic wars, denying their human feelings and their common sense, move back and forth across Europe slaughtering their fellows? "The war," Tolstoy answered, "was bound to happen simply because it was bound to happen." All prior history predetermined it. As for leaders, they, Tolstoy said, "are but the labels that serve to give a name to an end and, like labels, they have the least possible connection with the event." The greater the leader, "the more conspicuous the inevitability and the predestination of every act he commits." The leader, said Tolstoy, is "the slave of history."

Determinism takes many forms. Marxism is the determinism of class, Nazism the determinism of race. But the idea of men and women as the slaves of history runs athwart the deepest human instincts. Rigid determinism abolishes the idea of human freedom—the assumption of free choice that underlies every move we make, every word we speak, every thought we think. It abolishes the idea of human responsibility, since it is manifestly unfair to reward or punish people for actions that are by definition beyond their control. No one can live consistently by any deterministic creed. The Marxist states prove this themselves by their extreme susceptibility to the cult of leadership.

More than that, history refutes the idea that individuals make no difference. In December 1931 a British politician crossing Park Avenue in New York City between 76th and 77th Streets around ten-thirty at night looked in the wrong direction and was knocked down by an automobile—a moment, he later recalled, of a man aghast, a world aglare: "I do not understand why I was not broken like an eggshell or squashed like a gooseberry." Fourteen months later an American politician, sitting in an open car in Miami, Florida, was fired on by an assassin; the man beside him was hit. Those who believe that individuals make no difference to history might well ponder whether the next two decades would have been the same had Mario Contasini's car killed Winston Churchill in 1931 and Giuseppe Zangara's bullet killed Franklin Roosevelt in 1933. Suppose, in addition, that Adolf Hitler had been killed in the street fighting during the Munich *Putsch* of 1923 and that Lenin had died of typhus during the First World War. What would the 20th century be like now?

For better or for worse, individuals do make a difference. "The notion that a people can run itself and its affairs anonymously," wrote the philosopher William James, "is now well known to be the silliest of absurdities. Mankind does nothing save through initiatives on the part of inventors, great or small, and imitation by the rest of us—these are the sole factors in human progress. Individuals of genius show the way, and set the patterns, which common people then adopt and follow."

Leadership, James suggests, means leadership in thought as well as in action. In the long run, leaders in thought may well make the greater difference to the world. But, as Woodrow Wilson once said, "Those only are leaders of men, in the general eye, who lead in action. . . . It is at their hands that new thought gets its translation into the crude language of deeds." Leaders in thought often invent in solitude and obscurity, leaving to later generations the tasks of imitation. Leaders in action—the leaders portrayed in this series— have to be effective in their own time.

And they cannot be effective by themselves. They must act in response to the rhythms of their age. Their genius must be adapted, in a phrase of William James's, "to the receptivities of the moment." Leaders are useless without followers. "There goes the mob," said the French politician hearing a clamor in the streets. "I am their leader. I must follow them." Great leaders turn the inchoate emotions of the mob to purposes of their own. They seize on the opportunities of their time, the hopes, fears, frustrations, crises, potentialities.

They succeed when events have prepared the way for them, when the community is waiting to be aroused, when they can provide the clarifying and organizing ideas. Leadership ignites the circuit between the individual and the mass and thereby alters history.

It may alter history for better or for worse. Leaders have been responsible for the most extravagant follies and most monstrous crimes that have beset suffering humanity. They have also been vital in such gains as humanity has made in individual freedom, religious and racial tolerance, social justice and respect for human rights.

There is no sure way to tell in advance who is going to lead for good and who for evil. But a glance at the gallery of men and women in *World Leaders—Past and Present* suggests some useful tests.

One test is this: do leaders lead by force or by persuasion? By command or by consent? Through most of history leadership was exercised by the divine right of authority. The duty of followers was to defer and to obey. "Theirs not to reason why,/ Theirs but to do and die." On occasion, as with the so-called "enlightened despots" of the 18th century in Europe, absolutist leadership was animated by humane purposes. More often, absolutism nourished the passion for domination, land, gold and conquest and resulted in tyranny.

The great.revolution of modern times has been the revolution of equality. The idea that all people should be equal in their legal condition has undermined the old structures of authority, hierarchy and deference. The revolution of equality has had two contrary effects on the nature of leadership. For equality, as Alexis de Tocqueville pointed out in his great study *Democracy in America*, might mean equality in servitude as well as equality in freedom.

"I know of only two methods of establishing equality in the political world," Tocqueville wrote. "Rights must be given to every citizen, or none at all to anyone . . . save one, who is the master of all." There was no middle ground "between the sovereignty of all and the absolute power of one man." In his astonishing prediction of 20th-century totalitarian dictatorship, Tocqueville explained how the revolution of equality could lead to the "*Führerprinzip*" and more terrible absolutism than the world had ever known.

But when rights are given to every citizen and the sovereignty of all is established, the problem of leadership takes a new form, becomes more exacting than ever before. It is easy to issue commands and enforce them by the rope and the stake, the concentration camp and the *gulag*. It is much harder to use argument and achievement to overcome opposition and win consent. The Founding Fathers of the United States understood the difficulty. They believed that history had given them the opportunity to decide, as

Alexander Hamilton wrote in the first Federalist Paper, whether men are indeed capable of basing government on "reflection and choice, or whether they are forever destined to depend . . . on accident and force."

Government by reflection and choice called for a new style of leadership and a new quality of followership. It required leaders to be responsive to popular concerns, and it required followers to be active and informed participants in the process. Democracy does not eliminate emotion from politics; sometimes it fosters demagoguery; but it is confident that, as the greatest of democratic leaders put it, you cannot fool all of the people all of the time. It measures leadership by results and retires those who overreach or falter or fail.

It is true that in the long run despots are measured by results too. But they can postpone the day of judgment, sometimes indefinitely, and in the meantime they can do infinite harm. It is also true that democracy is no guarantee of virtue and intelligence in government, for the voice of the people is not necessarily the voice of God. But democracy, by assuring the rights of opposition, offers built-in resistance to the evils inherent in absolutism. As the theologian Reinhold Niebuhr summed it up, "Man's capacity for justice makes democracy possible, but man's inclination to injustice makes democracy necessary."

A second test for leadership is the end for which power is sought. When leaders have as their goal the supremacy of a master race or the promotion of totalitarian revolution or the acquisition and exploitation of colonies or the protection of greed and privilege or the preservation of personal power, it is likely that their leadership will do little to advance the cause of humanity. When their goal is the abolition of slavery, the liberation of women, the enlargement of opportunity for the poor and powerless, the extension of equal rights to racial minorities, the defense of the freedoms of expression and opposition, it is likely that their leadership will increase the sum of human liberty and welfare.

Leaders have done great harm to the world. They have also conferred great benefits. You will find both sorts in this series. Even "good" leaders must be regarded with a certain wariness. Leaders are not demigods; they put on their trousers one leg after another just like ordinary mortals. No leader is infallible, and every leader needs to be reminded of this at regular intervals. Irreverence irritates leaders but is their salvation. Unquestioning submission corrupts leaders and demeans followers. Making a cult of a leader is always a mistake. Fortunately hero worship generates its own antidote. "Every hero," said Emerson, "becomes a bore at last."

The signal benefit the great leaders confer is to embolden the rest of us to live according to our own best selves, to be active, insistent, and resolute in affirming our own sense of things. For great leaders attest to the reality of human freedom against the supposed inevitabilities of history. And they attest to the wisdom and power that may lie within the most unlikely of us, which is why Abraham Lincoln remains the supreme example of great leadership. A great leader, said Emerson, exhibits new possibilities to all humanity. "We feed on genius. . . . Great men exist that there may be greater men."

Great leaders, in short, justify themselves by emancipating and empowering their followers. So humanity struggles to master its destiny, remembering with Alexis de Tocqueville: "It is true that around every man a fatal circle is traced beyond which he cannot pass; but within the wide verge of that circle he is powerful and free; as it is with man, so with communities."

—*New York*

1
The Playboy

It was a hot summer day in Spain in 1799. A lean young Venezuelan boy was playing racketball with Prince Ferdinand of Asturias, the heir to the Spanish throne. It was a great honor for a colonial, and the prince showed that he knew it. The 17-year-old South American was a good player who played hard to win, but the prince, who knew that he was to be king of Spain one day, was not accustomed to being beaten.

They were evenly matched, and they played seriously and in silence as the Spanish court watched with amused interest. Neither took the lead for long, and the prince's face grew darker as he strained to put the boy from the colonies in his place. At one point the prince stumbled, and the Venezuelan's racket swept down and knocked his hat off. The prince angrily threw down his racket and called the game to a halt.

No one could knock the hat off a Spanish prince, and he demanded an apology. It had been an accident, but the royal honor had to be satisfied. The Venezuelan was not ready to apologize, however. It was true that he had been born in a Spanish colony, but he came from as old and distinguished a family as the young prince, and he was as used to receiving respect as anyone. If Prince Ferdinand didn't believe it had been an accident, the other was ready to fight.

Simón Bolívar in 1812, the year in which his failure to hold the Venezuelan city of Puerto Cabello against a Spanish siege provided him with a harsh incentive to master the art of war as quickly as possible.

Prince Ferdinand of Asturias (1784-1833). Ferdinand became king of Spain in 1808 and was promptly deposed by Emperor Napoleon of France. Following a six-year period during which Napoleon's brother, Joseph, had ruled the much-disputed country, Ferdinand regained the throne in 1814.

13

Before things got completely out of hand, the queen sided with the South American and told her son to stop being a crybaby. Ferdinand had no choice but to swallow his pride. The two returned to the game, and the incident was forgotten.

But it was a fateful encounter. Twenty years later the Venezuelan—Simón Bolívar—remembered it and recognized its meaning. By then, the two had played a more serious game than racketball and had fought over something more important than a hat. The Venezuelan boy was to shatter the Spanish empire and strip the future king of a continent.

Simón Bolívar (pronounced See-MONE Bo-LEE-var) was the son of one of the oldest and richest families in South America. The Bolívars were a noble Spanish family of Basque descent who had come to the New World more than two centuries before. There had been high-ranking officials among the Bolívars since they arrived in Venezuela in 1548, and when Simón was born in 1783, their holdings were immense. They owned the largest silver and copper mines in Venezuela, cattle ranches, and plantations of sugar, indigo, and cacao. From his mother's side had come land in Caracas and in the port city of La Guaira. Their estate in San Mateo alone contained more than 1,200 slaves. Young Simón was no less a prince in his own country than Ferdinand was in Spain.

But he was a creole—a native South American of European descent—and certain limitations came with membership in that class. Creoles could own property, but they were barred from holding the highest posts in government. They could engage in trade, but only under the strictest supervision of the mother country. They could amass personal fortunes, but they were heavily taxed.

Although they were the dominant class in the New World, their lives were strictly regulated from Spain, and the freedom their money and influence could buy was limited. Books could not be published or sold without the permission of the Spanish government, and education was kept to a minimum. Trade with other countries was not

permitted, and even trade between the colonies was severely regulated.

There were also tight restrictions on foreign travel, and only the wealthiest creoles could get around them. What perhaps galled the colonists most, however, was that they were without a voice in their own government; like the English colonists in North America a few years before, the Spanish in the New World had no representation in the government ruled by their European king.

Most creoles were loyal subjects of the king of Spain and thought of themselves as Spaniards. But the winds of revolution were in the air, blowing from the north and from Europe. The first shot of the American Revolution was fired in Lexington, Massachusetts in 1775, just eight years before Simón Bolívar's birth, and there is reason to believe that the "shot heard around the world" echoed not only in Europe, but south of the border. Already some creoles were beginning to think of themselves as Americans, rather than Spaniards.

When Simón was six, the French followed the North American example by storming the Bastille and deposing their king. In the next 30 years South America was to undergo an upheaval greater

The royal palace in Madrid, Spain, in 1800. At the time of young Simón Bolívar's visit in 1799, Madrid had a population of 200,000 and contained not only the greatest concentration of royal and noble palaces in Spain, but also many universities and libraries.

Charles IV of Spain (1748-1819). Unduly influenced by his ambitious wife, Queen María Luisa, Charles IV showed during his reign a weakness of character which resulted in Spain's loss of national sovereignty when the emperor of France, Napoleon Bonaparte, forced Charles to abdicate in May 1808.

than anything North America or Europe had ever seen, and Simón Bolívar, the rich, privileged, young gentleman of Caracas, was to be at the head of it all. He was to prove himself a military leader and statesman of genius. Called "the George Washington of South America," he was to become the father of not one but five countries.

He could not have been born to a life of more ease and luxury. Though the condition of the Spanish colonists was restricted in some ways, the wealthy lived the good life with as much refinement and gusto as their European relations. The abundant lands of the New World provided rich and varied food and wine, and the most elegant fashions in clothes were available to those who could afford them. Music and literature were seriously cultivated, and every kind of sport known in Europe was enjoyed.

Simón was the youngest of four children, always loved and pampered by his brother and two sisters. As befits a young prince, he had the best of everything, and enjoyed it all thoroughly. His father, 57 years old when Simón was born, had little influence on him. An elegant and cultured dandy, he died when the boy was three. His mother died six years later, leaving the young boy to be brought up by his uncle in a house full of servants. His nurse, Hipólita, was the closest thing to a real parent he ever had. All his life he remembered the love and devotion of this black slave. And years later, shortly

A meeting between Spanish *conquistadores* (conquerors) and Peruvian Indians, as portrayed by the British painter H. P. Briggs. Peru remained the most conservative Spanish colony in South America until the early 19th century, when Simón Bolívar liberated the country.

A 19th-century engraving portraying (l. to r.): the Botocudos of Brazil; the natives of Patagonia; and the natives of Tierra del Fuego. The 16th-century Spanish invaders often dealt harshly with the native peoples, forcing them to bow to Spanish political and religious institutions.

before his death, he referred to her in a letter to one of his sisters as "my mother Hipólita" and said, "give her everything she wishes. . . . She nourished my life. I know no other parent but her."

In those days elementary education, such as it was, was left to priests and private tutors in the New World. Young Simón was evidently quite a handful. He preferred horseback riding to Latin grammar and dancing to ancient history. A bundle of energy, he wore out his tutors with his boisterous spirit. "You're a keg of dynamite," one of his tutors exclaimed to him. "Then don't come near me," was the boy's quick response. "I might explode."

Although Simón loved to read—*Don Quixote* was his favorite book and he carried it everywhere—none of his teachers succeeded in instilling him with any discipline as a student. He was hardly able to write when he met his last and most important tutor, a man whose influence was to shape his thought for life.

Simón Rodríguez was an eccentric, to say the least. Only 11 years older than his nine-year-old student, he had already tramped through Spain, France, and Germany and read all the philosophy he could lay his hands on. He never stayed long in one place—partly because he usually got in trouble chasing women or spouting radical philosophy, and

Socially prominent Peruvians attend a ball in Lima, their capital city, c. 1820.

The French revolutionary Georges Danton delivers an address in 1792. A clever politician and devoted republican, Danton, who emphasized a practical and human approach to the politics of revolution, is remembered as a moderate. Bolívar too, in the course of his revolutionary career, while not afraid to fight, strongly disapproved of unnecessary violence.

partly because he was a rover. "I don't want to be like a tree, always rooted to one spot," he said.

Of all the philosophers Rodríguez had read, the one that impressed him most was the Frenchman Jean-Jacques Rousseau, whose ideas of "the natural man" were much in fashion in Europe. Rousseau wrote that man was by nature good but was corrupted by civilization, and he urged a return to the life of nature. To many his ideas were dangerous: he argued that all people were naturally free and equal. "Man is born free," he wrote in *The Social Contract*, "and everywhere he is in chains."

Rousseau's opposition to authority was also expressed in his theory of education. He wrote that to keep a child's mind in a state of nature he should be allowed to develop without interference. "I hate books," Rousseau wrote, "they teach how to talk of what one does not know . . . reading is childhood's curse."

Rodríguez adopted this philosophy completely and trained young Simón to think and act naturally without filling his mind with a lot of useless information. He taught him to observe keenly and to act on his observations. They moved from Caracas to the country, and rode, swam, and hiked together.

Slaves on a plantation in Brazil during the 19th century. Slavery was a major component of national economies throughout the Americas from the 16th century until the mid-19th, when liberals such as Bolívar began to realize that there was no place in a true republic for a cruel system such as slavery.

A 19th-century German artist's impression of Don Quixote, the literary creation of Miguel de Cervantes (1547-1616). Many of Simón Bolívar's friends considered his character similar to that of Don Quixote, whom Cervantes portrayed as both an opponent of injustice and a mix of martyr, hero, and dreamer.

The title page of *Emile*, a treatise on education by the philosopher Jean-Jacques Rousseau (1712-1778).

ÉMILE,

O U

DE L'ÉDUCATION.

Par J. J. ROUSSEAU,

Citoyen de Genève.

Sanabilibus ægrotamus malis; ipſaque nós in rectum
genitos natura, ſi emendari velimus, juvat.
Sen: de ird. L. II. c. 13.

TOME PREMIER.

A AMSTERDAM,

Chez JEAN NÉAULME, Libraire.

M. DCC. LXII.

Avec Privilége de Noſſeigneurs les Etats
de Hollande & de Weſtfriſe.

Faksimile des Titels der erſten Ausgabe von
Rouſſeaus „Emile". Originalgröße.

Jean-Jacques Rousseau, the French philosopher whose teachings greatly influenced Simón Rodríguez, Bolívar's tutor. Rousseau's political philosophy (which inspired republican leaders throughout the 19th century) declared that while people might *grant* their government sovereignty over the affairs of state, such sovereignty should remain the *undisputed and inalienable property* of the people.

The boy's rather frail body hardened, and his eager mind quickened. He was the ideal student of which Rousseau might have dreamed. Years later Rodríguez wrote of him, "He knew more by intuition than I by meditation and study."

This carefree life lasted five years. Then in 1797 Rodríguez got in trouble again—this time for something really serious. He was involved in an attempted revolution.

Uprisings against Spanish rule were nothing new in the colonies. There had been one in Venezuela in 1731, and many other colonies had had them too. The Spanish put them down with savage firmness. In 1780, for example, an Indian leader, convicted of revolutionary activity in Peru, was dragged by a horse to the main plaza of Cuzco and held while his wife and children were killed before his eyes. Then his tongue was torn out—for speaking against the king of Spain—and he was tied to four horses and pulled to pieces. His body was burned and his head displayed on a spike, as a warning for anyone tempted to follow his example.

Miguel de Cervantes, author of *Don Quixote*, a novel which Simón Bolívar loved to read when he was a child. The hero of the story, Don Quixote, was a Spanish knight with a vivid and romantic imagination who always acted in accordance with his convictions.

Such horrible punishments kept most of the residents—Indian and Spanish colonial alike—from doing anything about their grievances. But occasionally dissatisfaction erupted. In 1797 two creole intellectuals organized a plan to overthrow the Spanish rule of Venezuela. An informer reported the plot, and the government acted swiftly to spread a dragnet. One of the leaders, Manuel Gual, escaped, but the other, José María de España, was caught, dragged to the gallows, and his head and limbs hacked from his body and put on public display.

Rodríguez was narrowly acquitted but kept under watch. It was obviously time to leave Venezuela. "Wind, water, sun—" he had said, "everything that moves and is never still—that's the life for me." He boarded a British ship and continued his world travels.

Simón was 14 and at loose ends. Earlier his father had organized a militia battalion and Simón joined as a cadet. There is little reason to believe he got any real military training from this band of toy soldiers, but he had a chance to parade on week-

The plaza and cathedral in Lima, the capital of Peru. The conservative Spanish political system remained more powerful in Peru than anywhere else in South America, and few members of either the ruling classes or the general population considered Spain their oppressor when José de San Martín partially liberated the country in 1821.

ends and wear a dress uniform. He stayed with it a year and was promoted to the rank of lieutenant because of his family name.

Caracas was at his feet. Bright, intelligent, elegant, good looking, and rich, he was a great success with the women. He loved dancing, swimming, riding, and dueling, and was expert at all of them. A life of ease and pleasure seemed clearly marked out for him.

But there was a restlessness in the young Simón Bolívar which the family noticed with some alarm. He enjoyed his life as a young dandy, but it didn't seem to satisfy him. His tutor had given him idealistic theories, but the events of 1797 which had forced Rodríguez to flee forced Simón to look at the realities of politics for the first time. Perhaps the wide avenues of Caracas, and even the wide plains of Venezuela, were beginning to seem confining to him.

It was obvious to his family, at any rate, that he had nothing more to learn at home. A trip overseas seemed the answer, and, as the family had influential relatives in Spain, they arranged to send the boy over to complete his education in the old country. Perhaps he could make his fortune as well. And so in January 1799 the 15-year-old Simón Bolívar set sail for Spain.

During a brief stop-over in Mexico Simón spent almost all of his money and raised a few eyebrows with talk of liberty, justice, equality, and revolution. But no one took the words of a young playboy from Venezuela very seriously.

He arrived late in the spring, near his 16th birthday, determined to see what Spain had to offer him. If he thought of freedom for his country, it was still only an idea, not a practical possibility. He was trying his wings, on his own for the first time. The young provincial prince had come to confront the haughty old world of Europe.

An interior view of Simón Bolívar's house in Caracas.

2

The Idealist

The dashing young man from the colonies was an immediate success in Spain. Letters from his family gained him entry to the highest circles, and he was at home with the best families of Madrid. King Charles IV and his queen, María Luisa, ruled the society of the capital as they did the country—with style and elegance but with a moral laxity that made them the scandal of Europe. Charles' cabinet minister, Manuel de Godoy, "the Prince of Peace," was well known to be the queen's lover, and the contempt their behavior inspired among Europeans was not lost on the young Bolívar. Whatever respect he may have brought with him for the Spanish royal house, or for the institution of monarchy in general, he lost it during that first year. It was then that he saw how the future king behaved on the racketball court.

It wasn't long, in such an atmosphere, before romance struck the young Bolívar. Almost at once he fell in love with the daughter of one of the first families of Madrid. María Teresa de Toro, 20 months older than he, was a gentle and charming girl. She was not a great beauty but her spirit and maturity made her a great favorite with everyone. He courted her with tenderness and passion, and she returned his love fully. He humbly asked her family for her hand.

Napoleon Bonaparte, emperor of France from 1804 to 1814. A political radical at the time of the French Revolution, his coup d'etat of 1799 destroyed the institutions of the revolutionary government.

A street scene in Paris, shortly before the revolution of 1789. When elections in 1797 showed lingering popular support for a constitutional monarchy, the stage was set for the reactionary coup of November 10, 1799, when Napoleon Bonaparte seized power and laid the foundations for his future imperial career.

King Charles IV of Spain and his family, as portrayed by the artist Francisco Goya (1746-1828). Like Bolívar, Goya sympathized with the republican response to regal despotism in early 19th-century Spain. A supporter of the French intervention (1808-1813), Goya left Spain in 1814 despite his reinstatement as court painter, and died in France in 1828.

The de Toros were sympathetic to the marriage—the handsome, accomplished son of one of the richest families in South America was a good catch, even in Spain—but they felt the 17-year-old boy was a little too young. So they set a condition. If he agreed to spend a year traveling in Europe and afterwards they both still wanted to marry, they could. He agreed and in 1801 set off for Paris.

France had just come through the bloodbath of its revolution, and Napoleon was first consul. It was a time of great prosperity and progress, and Bolívar saw dramatized some of the ideas of the rights of man Rodríguez had planted in his mind. He could not help being impressed by a country where a man could become head of state through merit rather than family. Napoleon was the hero of the hour, and no one admired him more than the young Venezuelan.

But Bolívar's thoughts were more with his bride-to-be, and the political conditions of France probably made little impression on him. His letters home at the time were devoted largely to requests for money. "My head," he wrote later, "was only filled with the mists of a passionate love." At last the year passed, and in 1802 he returned, married María Teresa, and carried her off to Venezuela.

He was the happiest man alive—young, rich, and in love. He saw an uninterrupted future of peace and leisure on one of his estates and beside his beloved wife. Then tragedy struck. After ten months of idyllic happiness, María Teresa contracted and was killed by a tropical fever, and Bolívar was alone again. Not yet 21, he had lost his parents and his wife, and he was left without an heir. Perhaps, as a South American orator declared, these tragedies

Spanish statesman Manuel de Godoy (1767-1851). Godoy was imprisoned by Charles IV for the disastrous results of his pro-French policies. His career reflects the opportunism and corruption in 19th-century Spanish politics which Bolívar so detested.

An overseer, accompanied by two slaves, patrols a plantation in Venezuela during the early 19th century. Black slaves in Venezuela numbered around 70,000 at this time. The country also contained thousands of freed slaves, some of whom were refugees from French islands in the Caribbean. The Venezuelan government automatically granted such refugees their freedom.

were necessary to free him for work impossible to men with close personal obligations. "Neither Washington nor Bolívar was destined to have children of his own," declared Atilano Carnevali as he placed a wreath before Washington's statue in Caracas in 1920, "so that we Americans might call ourselves their children." Bolívar admitted later that if his wife had lived he would have become the mayor of San Mateo and would never have taken on the struggle for independence.

Life in Venezuela was impossible for Bolívar now. Everything reminded him of María, and the role of a country gentleman, managing cacao plantations in the colonies, was intolerable. He decided to return to Europe. Perhaps a change of scene would relieve his despair and give him a new direction.

But Spain was not the answer either. The life of a colonial playboy among Spanish aristocrats was as distasteful to him as that of a gentleman planter in Venezuela, and Madrid was as full of painful memories of María Teresa as Caracas. Above all, he was still a creole—not really a first-class citizen of Spain—and his lesser status rankled him.

It was dramatically brought home to him almost

at once. With the excuse of a threatened food shortage, the government issued a rule expelling all foreigners—and Simón Bolívar was considered a foreigner. If the poorest native laborer had rights he lacked, it was with little regret that he turned his back on Spain. And he never went back.

Paris was the obvious choice. "The City of Lights," so lively and progressive, was the capital of Europe then, and Napoleon the greatest name. Bolívar threw himself into the social and intellectual life of the city. He found a distant cousin, Fanny du Villars, who had social gatherings of all the best minds of Paris, and Bolívar became a regular in her salon. (Most historians agree that he was also a regular guest in her bedroom.)

It was in the salon of his charming "cousin" that he met the philosophers, the writers, and the wits of Paris, and it was probably there that he first met Alexander von Humboldt, the most famous explorer and scientist of his day. Humboldt was the first to

A court of the Spanish Inquisition prepares to torture a heretic. The politically conservative Catholic Church, a major social force in South America throughout the revolutionary period in the early 19th century, was respected by liberals (such as Bolívar) and royalists.

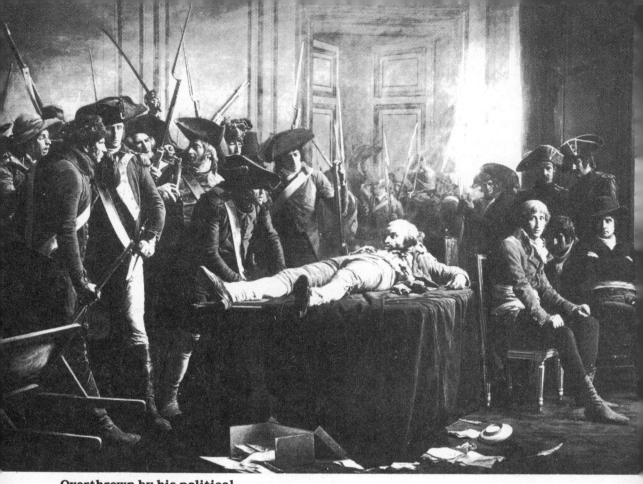

make a really accurate description of Bolívar's homeland, so naturally the two had things to talk about. The older man was taken with Bolívar immediately, and they met often.

One day the talk turned to the political situation of Bolívar's land. "I believe Venezuela is ready for independence," Humboldt declared, "but where is the man strong enough to bring it about?" The question was a fateful one. Perhaps it ignited a spark in Bolívar. Years later he told a friend that he had left the scientist's study that night "very thoughtful." No one can know exactly what lit the fire in the mind of the young man, but it is clear that during this time a new sense of purpose was growing in him. He was beginning to realize that liberty would not come about by wishing for it or talking about it. It had to be achieved. Somebody had to *bring it about.*

Napoleon Bonaparte, the former republican whose later assumption of imperial status so disgusted Simón Bolívar, invades the chambers of the Council of the Five Hundred on November 10, 1799, thus ending France's experiment in parliamentary government.

Bonaparte, as the first consul was still known, was gradually expanding his authority. It was becoming increasingly clear that, with the willing consent of most of the public, he was becoming more and more a monarch, and France less and less a republic. At last, in 1804, he made it official and had himself declared emperor.

Though many had seen it coming, the ceremony came as a great blow to others. Beethoven, who had dedicated his third symphony, the *Eroica* or "Heroic," to Napoleon, struck out the dedication on the score with a savage stroke of his pen. Bolívar was no less disgusted. He felt betrayed. The great republican Bonaparte had deserted his ideals. In declaring himself Emperor Napoleon I, he had seized power like any ancient tyrant.

In rage and despair, Bolívar refused the invitation to watch the coronation from the box of the Spanish embassy. He felt a sense of personal loss, as at the death of a parent or a friend. He had lost a hero.

Napoleon Bonaparte is crowned emperor of France on December 2, 1804. Although dismayed by the anti-republican nature of the event, Simón Bolívar, looking back in his later years on a series of collapsed republican constitutions in South America, came to believe that dictatorship might better guarantee political stability.

The title page of the score of Beethoven's *Third Symphony*. The savagery with which the composer erased the dedication to Napoleon in 1804 is clearly visible.

Ludwig van Beethoven (1770-1827), the German composer who in 1804 struck the dedication to Napoleon from the score of his *Third Symphony*. Prior to Napoleon's coronation, Beethoven, like many European intellectuals, had thought the French leader a true liberal who might change the face of a Europe stifled by conservatism.

Alexander von Humboldt (1769-1859), the German naturalist and statesman whom Bolívar met in Paris in 1804. Some historians believe that Humboldt had an even better appreciation of the political situation in Spanish America than Bolívar himself did.

His spirits lifted when he learned that his old tutor, Rodríguez, was in Europe living under the name of Robinson (taken from Robinson Crusoe, the castaway in Daniel Defoe's novel—Rodriguez' favorite character and Rousseau's model of the natural man). After living in a few countries, including the United States for three years, "Robinson" had found a job in Vienna in the laboratory of a famous chemist. Bolívar sent for him at once. Here was exactly the companion he needed.

The two friends decided to go on a tour to discuss their anger and disappointment with Napoleon. They made a pilgrimage to Rousseau's home, crossed the Alps, and at last found their way to Italy.

Italy, the cradle of liberty and the source of Roman law which was the basis of all republican ideas, was the natural end of their wanderings. Bolívar saw Napoleon crowned again at Marengo—he couldn't resist his second chance at the spectacle, though he spoke so openly against the emperor that Rodríguez had to hurry him out of the crowd for fear of being arrested.

At last they reached Rome. They visited every part, the new and the old, fascinated by this living monument to the human spirit. One day after dinner they climbed Monte Sacro, the "Sacred Mountain," in the north of the city. While only a small hill, Monte Sacro has a special place in history. It was here that the plebians, the poor commoners of ancient Rome, fled from the oppression of the patricians and nobles 2,000 years earlier. Here the com-

Religion is the law of conscience. Any law that imposes it negates it, because to apply compulsion to conscience is to destroy the value of faith, which is the very essence of religion. The sacred... doctrines are useful, enlightening, and spiritually nourishing. We should all avow them, but the obligation is moral rather than political.
—SIMÓN BOLÍVAR
in a letter concerning his proposals for a constitution for Bolivia

Daniel Defoe (1659-1731), the English writer and author of *Robinson Crusoe*, the novel whose shipwrecked hero provided the French philosopher Rousseau with a model for his ideal "natural man," and Rodríguez, Bolívar's tutor, with a favorite literary character.

mon man asserted his equality and his right to freedom, just as the North Americans had done in 1776 and the French in 1789. The model for the United States Declaration of Independence and the French Declaration of the Rights of Man had originated here, on Monte Sacro. The patrician Simón Bolívar was profoundly moved. A turning point in his life had arrived, and he knew his mission. As Rodríguez recounted it, many years later:

"He turned toward me, away from Rome. His eyes were moist, and he was breathing heavily as if with fever. He said: 'I swear before you, by the God of my fathers and the honor of my country: I will not rest, not in body or soul, till I have broken the chains of Spain.' "

Columbus had been the discoverer of the New World; Cortéz had been the conqueror; Simón Bolívar dedicated himself to be the liberator, and it is as *El Libertador* that he is known in South America to this day.

A view of Rome in the early 19th century. Some historians have suggested that Bolívar's exposure to the spectacular ceremonies of imperial France, followed by a visit to Rome, an ancient seat of authoritarian republicanism, provoked in him an initially unconscious ambition for personal power which only became fully apparent later.

A view of Rome from the tower of St. Peter's.

SIMON BOLIVAR.

3

The Firebrand

> *To unite merely to sleep was a disgrace yesterday. Today it is treason!...Let us lay the cornerstone of liberty without fear. To hesitate is to die!*
> —SIMÓN BOLÍVAR
> in a speech at Caracas in 1811

While Bolívar the passionate idealist was just beginning to understand the practical problems of making a revolution, others were trying to do something about them.

The most famous of all the older revolutionaries was Francisco de Miranda, a man who just would not quit. Born in Caracas in 1750, Miranda had held a commission in the Spanish army. But he became obsessed with the idea of freeing Venezuela, and barely escaped arrest by the Spanish. He traveled everywhere, earning a great reputation as a soldier and a lover. In the French Revolution he won the rank of brigadier general. Catherine the Great gave him a commission in the Russian army (though it was said he earned it in her private chambers rather than on the battlefield). British prime minister William Pitt put him on the foreign office payroll.

Everywhere he went, he tried to get support for his dream of a free Venezuela. And everywhere people sympathized but backed away from any real involvement. England, France, Russia, the United States—they all gave him moral support and a little money now and then, but no one wanted to get involved in anything as dangerous as a revolution.

At last in February 1806, he managed to round up 180 recruits in New York, paid out of his own pocket, and set off to invade South America.

Simón Bolívar wearing full military dress uniform. Such uniform was permitted to persons of high standing in early 19th-century Spanish society.

General Francisco Miranda (1750?-1816), the Venezuelan soldier whose career ended in 1812, when his capture by the Spanish signalled the fall of the First Venezuelan Republic.

41

The expedition was a disaster from the beginning. The Spanish, who got wind of it in advance, were waiting for him and never let him get near the shore. Two of his three ships were sunk, and a third of his men captured. Miranda himself barely escaped.

But nothing discouraged him. Six months later he tried again, this time with money borrowed from sympathizers in the United States. He was convinced that once he landed, Venezuelans would rally to him and sweep the Spanish out. He knew he was in for a fight, but he was sure he would win.

He was ready for anything—except what he found. He got ashore all right; he landed at Coro, just as he had planned, and found—nothing!

The port city was deserted. The citizens had all run out. Miranda raised a new flag and proclaimed the birth of a new republic, but nobody was there to see or hear it. He waited for his countrymen to

Francisco Miranda languishes in a Spanish jail following his capture in 1812 and the fall of the First Venezuelan Republic. Miranda's career as an opponent of Spanish rule in South America began in the 1770s, when he visited the United States and first studied the political institutions of democracy.

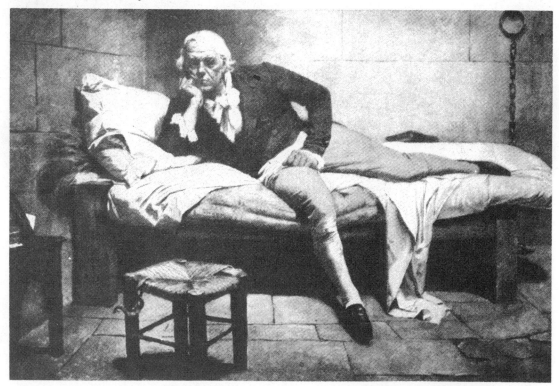

come back and take their liberty from his hands. Yet what he received was the information that there was a price on his head, that native troops were on their way to arrest him, and that everyone considered him a traitor. "The Venezuelans would have nothing to do with us," one of his men wrote later. "They refused our offer of liberty."

Miranda's mistake was that he really did not know how the Venezuelans felt about things. He had not set foot on Venezuelan soil for 35 years. He thought that because there had been Indian and slave uprisings, the Spanish-American population was ready to rise up and take charge of their own land. But in fact, most of his countrymen remained loyal to their king in spite of everything. The creoles would have to be won over to his way of thinking before he could accomplish anything by force. In disgust (and fearing for his life), Miranda set sail for England.

Bolívar had left Rodríguez in Italy, in the meantime, and returned to Paris. But the Old World had nothing more to teach him, and in 1806, when he heard of Miranda's heroic—and slightly crazy— effort, he knew his course.

He left for Venezuela at once and arrived early in 1807—a new man with new ideas. He was 24, and he knew exactly where he was going in life.

He already understood Miranda's problem better than the old soldier did himself. He knew his job was to bring his people around, to stir them up, to get them ready for a revolution. Then, and only then, would a revolution be possible.

As the son of one of the most prominent families in Caracas, and as a man who had just returned from seeing Napoleon, meeting the king of Spain, and playing in Paris, he was in demand everywhere. His wealth, charm, and good looks had always made him popular, and now he was the man of the hour. He was invited everywhere, and quietly set about spreading the word. He met all the right people. He organized dances and gave brilliant parties, all the time building an underground movement and waiting for the right moment.

The hour came sooner than anyone expected, and

A British cartoon of 1808 ridicules Napoleon Bonaparte and his brother, Joseph, whom Napoleon had made king of Spain in an attempt to consolidate the French empire. The intervention proved disastrous to Napoleon's military efforts elsewhere in Europe, since the suppression of the Spanish people required the stationing of thousands of French troops throughout the country.

British troops under Lord Wellington assaulting a French artillery position in Spain in 1810. Wellington, known as the "Iron Duke," was a brilliant strategist who set standards in military efficiency which greatly influenced a generation of revolutionary generals in Spanish America, especially José de San Martín, the liberator of both Argentina and Peru.

Bolívar recognized it at once. Ironically, it was Napoleon—the man Bolívar saw as betraying the cause of independence—who opened the door for him. In his thirst for power, Napoleon gave the New World the chance for which it was waiting.

In 1808 Napoleon began to pour soldiers into Spain and pressured the weak King Charles into abdicating. Napoleon then placed his brother Joseph on the Spanish throne.

The Spanish were furious: at Napoleon for taking the throne, and at Charles for giving it to him. They set up an opposition government and proclaimed Charles' son their rightful king, Ferdinand VII.

The rebellion against Napoleon and his brother Joseph was crushed ferociously. On the day after the uprising, the infamous Third of May still mourned by the Spanish, hundreds of civilians were lined up indiscriminately and shot. But the Spanish refused to give in, and local assemblies, called *juntas*, sprang up everywhere, claiming authority in the name of King Ferdinand VII. A guerrilla war—liberally aided by the English, who had their own war going against the French—broke out.

If the Spanish suffered from conflicting loyalties, the colonies were even more confused. The Spanish officials in the New World continued to take orders from Madrid, but now they were getting two sets of orders—one set from the "official" government, which was French, and one set from the rebels who supported the uncrowned Ferdinand VII. Most of the creoles, the landowning and professional class, supported Ferdinand.

I am less inclined toward the federal form of government. Such a system is no more than organized anarchy, or, at best, a law that implicitly prescribes the obligation of dissolution and the eventual ruin of the state. I think it would be better for South America to adopt the Koran [the sacred book of the Moslem faith] rather than the United States' form of government, although the latter is the best on earth.
—SIMÓN BOLÍVAR
in a letter to General Daniel O'Leary, one of his most trusted aides, on September 13, 1829

Napoleon Bonaparte, the French emperor whose occupation of Spain in 1808 enabled liberals throughout Spanish America to plan for independence.

45

There were two reasons for the creoles to support Ferdinand VII: first, they felt genuine loyalty to the royal family of Bourbon (although the Bourbons were historically not Spanish at all, but French); second, the liberal creoles saw a chance in all the confusion to get out from under foreign rule altogether.

Revolutionary *juntas* began to appear all over South America, all claiming to be for Ferdinand VII. There were assemblies in Caracas, Bogotá, Quito, and La Paz in the North, and Buenos Aires at the other end of the continent. The liberals were hoping to free their colonies, and the conservatives were trying to preserve their ties with the government—and of course hold on to their own property.

Bolívar saw the chaos and knew the time was ripe for action. If the people would not accept a French puppet as their king and could not look for authority from Ferdinand in exile, they would have no choice but to stand on their own feet. And none knew better than Bolívar that even if Ferdinand

A statue of Simón Bolívar in Caracas, Venezuela.

did get into power he would be an unstable king. A boy who had acted like a baby on a racketball court was not the man to rule a worldwide empire. With his brother Juan, his in-laws the de Toros, and some trusted friends, Bolívar set up a secret society in his home. He stayed on good terms with the Spanish government at Caracas, but he worked actively for independence. When cautioned by the Marqués de Casa León that he and his friends were playing a dangerous game, he stated his position boldly: "We have declared war on Spain."

Of course the government kept him under watch, but the rich young planter was not taken very seriously. Venezuela's new governor, Vincente de Emparán, got to know him personally—or thought he did—and laughed off his talk of national independence. Emparán was a clever man. His personal charm and good nature made him seem like a reasonable, friendly fellow, but he acted swiftly and severely. He sent many suspected men into exile, made it a criminal act to receive printed

British and French troops fight it out at the Battle of Talavera in Spain in 1809, the year in which Vincente de Emparán arrived in Caracas to assume the position of governor of Venezuela. Emparán relinquished his authority on April 19, 1810, when Bolívar and other prominent Venezuelans asked him to resign.

material from overseas, and set up a spy system. Bolívar knew it was just a matter of time before Emparán would break up his secret society and have him arrested.

And the news from Spain was getting worse. The opposition government, the central *junta*, was having trouble staying out of the hands of Napoleon's army, and there were even rumors that it had disbanded. Bolívar's revolutionary group agreed it was time to make a move.

On April 19, 1810—35 years to the day after the battle of Lexington, which marked the beginning of the American Revolution—a group of rebels approached Emparán on his way into church and said it was necessary to form a representative council of Venezuelans to govern the country. Emparán said he would consider it. But it was too late to play for time. The rebels said he must go with them at once to the council chamber.

Emparán looked to his troops though and saw there was no help to be had from them. Official pride was one thing, but these rebels looked dangerous, and the governor was no fool. He went with them.

In the chamber they informed him calmly that he could no longer remain as governor of Venezuela. Emparán responded with dignity. "Let the people decide," he said, and stepped out on the balcony to ask the crowd below if they wanted him to stay. It was a gamble, of course, and he must have known it. The fate of Venezuela hung in the balance for a moment, and then the people in the street began to shout "No!" It was all over. The revolution had started, and its first battle was won. Three centuries of Spanish rule in South America had come to an end.

Like the first shot fired at Lexington and "heard 'round the world," the events of this spring morning in Caracas resounded throughout South America. The capital of every Spanish colony in the New World, except Peru and Guatemala, followed the example within six months: Buenos Aires on May 25, Bogotá on July 26, Chile and Ecuador in September.

Thomas Paine, the British-born radical writer whose republican ideas exerted great influence on European and American revolutionaries in the late 18th and early 19th centuries.

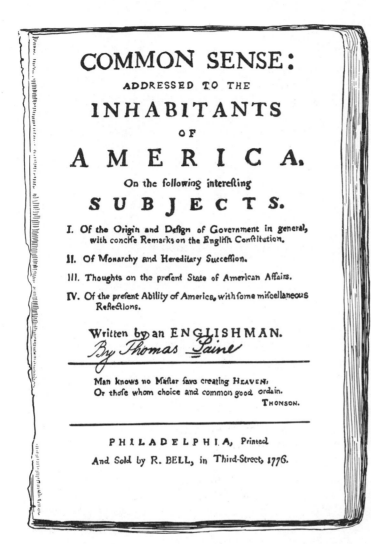

COMMON SENSE:

ADDRESSED TO THE

INHABITANTS

OF

AMERICA.

On the following interesting

SUBJECTS.

I. Of the Origin and Design of Government in general, with concise Remarks on the English Constitution.

II. Of Monarchy and Hereditary Succession.

III. Thoughts on the present State of American Affairs.

IV. Of the present Ability of America, with some miscellaneous Reflections.

Written by an ENGLISHMAN.

By Thomas Paine

Man knows no Master save creating HEAVEN, Or those whom choice and common good ordain.
THOMSON.

PHILADELPHIA, Printed
And Sold by R. BELL, in Third-Street, 1776.

The title page of *Common Sense*, the 1776 pamphlet which urged the immediate declaration of American independence from Great Britain. Its author, Thomas Paine, a British radical, later wrote *The Rights of Man*, which the British authorities considered so seditious that they decided to outlaw Paine in 1792.

William Pitt (1759-1806), the British foreign secretary who for many years closely followed the emergence of Spanish-American separatist movements and often understood the complexities of the situation much better than the revolutionaries themselves.

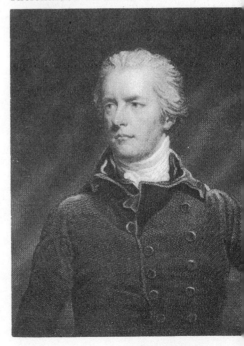

It was not all clear sailing, of course. Not everyone went along with the overthrow. But it began well. The first decisions of the new *junta* were moderate and just: they expelled Emparán and other Spanish authorities, courteously but firmly; and they liberalized the laws by abolishing the monetary tribute due from Indians. The introduction of slaves was also abolished. Then they began to organize a truly representative government like that of their neighbor to the north, the United States.

Everyone knew that it was important for the new *junta* to be recognized by other governments, so

Conquistadores torture a South American Indian during the 16th-century Spanish invasion of the continent. Such actions against the native population, while prevalent in the initial conquests, did not last long, since the Spanish authorities considered the Indians subjects of the Spanish monarch and thus entitled to fair treatment.

one of the first acts of the new *junta* was to send diplomatic representatives to other colonies and countries to ask for recognition and help. Some of the diplomats were ignored—the United States, for example, did not want to mix in Spanish affairs—and some were even jailed as traitors. But others were well treated and successful. Among the less successful was Simón Bolívar, who headed the mission to England.

Bolívar was not the leader of the Venezuelan revolution, for at this time there was no one who stood out above all the rest. But he was one of the most active, intelligent, and determined. And he was one of the richest. The diplomatic mission to England would never have existed if Bolívar had not offered to pick up the bill for it.

Officially Venezuela was still a Spanish colony, loyal to its rightful king, Ferdinand VII. Thus far the revolution had been only to throw off the rule of France and to allow the people to run their own country till the king was restored. This, of course, the English accepted gladly; Napoleon and the French were their enemy too. But Bolívar—for all his pleading, for all the propaganda he wrote for the English papers—could not persuade the English government to recognize what he really wanted—

50

a free, independent Venezuela. They treated him with courtesy and sympathy, but the English were too cautious to give any promises of real support. As long as Spain was her ally, England would never back a rebel *junta.*

The mission, while not a diplomatic success, did accomplish one important thing. It brought back Miranda.

One of the first things Bolívar did when he arrived in London was to look up the legendary old general. Miranda, now 60, had been living there since his two unsuccessful revolutionary expeditions to Venezuela four years before. He had written a steady stream of passionate propaganda for a free Venezuela, and generally made as much of a nuisance of himself as he could to the Spanish. There was a huge price on his head in Spain, and the *junta* back in Caracas had specifically warned Bolívar to have nothing to do with him. If they became involved with this old hawk, they could never pretend they were loyally waiting for Ferdinand to come back and take over.

But Bolívar had his own ideas about that, and straightaway asked Miranda to come home. With-

A court of the Spanish Inquisition holds a heresy trial during the 17th century. Despite its close association with the Spanish crown, the Church retained its prestige in the eyes of both liberals and conservatives throughout the revolutionary period in Spanish America. In 1830 Bolívar's final appeal for Colombian unity stressed the importance of religion.

Parliament House in London, England. At the time of Bolívar's visit to London in 1810, Britain's foreign affairs chiefs were aware of the separatist sentiments which many Spanish Americans harbored beneath their apparent loyalty to Ferdinand VII of Spain, the exiled king who did not regain his throne until 1814.

out a moment's hesitation, the old revolutionary said yes.

Miranda got a hero's welcome in some quarters, though there were many people who were not so glad to see the old agitator. He was made a lieutenant general in the army, but it was just a symbolic gesture since there was no real army. He was a great name but not a very popular man.

He was just what Bolívar needed, however, to back him up in his efforts. Between the two of them—the famous old soldier and the hot young firebrand—the public sentiment in favor of independence became overwhelming. No one could resist Bolívar's oratory; his passionate delivery could stir up a crowd to do anything.

On April 19, 1811, the anniversary of the expulsion of Governor Emparán, there were parades in Caracas and a statue of Ferdinand was pulled down. The yeast Bolívar had added to society had begun to rise. "Today is the anniversary of our revolution," wrote a newspaper that day. "May the first year of independence and freedom now begin."

Bolívar's "Patriotic Society," as his once secret organization was now called, held stormier and more public meetings. It has been said that nothing is as powerful as an idea whose time has come. But an idea is powerless without a man to promote

Ferdinand VII of Spain (1784-1833). Ferdinand, declared the rightful king of Spain by the Spanish people in 1808 (in opposition to Joseph Bonaparte, Napoleon's brother), proved a reactionary and despotic monarch who fully favored the brutal methods employed by his generals in suppressing liberal revolutions in South America.

Bolívar's residence in Caracas, photographed during the 1930s, when Venezuela had become the world's second greatest producer, and leading exporter, of oil. It is ironic that much of the wealth thus gained by Venezuela, birthplace of Bolívar the liberator, was used at that time to finance increased repression of the Venezuelan people by the army and police.

A 19th-century lithograph showing the course of the Thames River through London. The apparent loyalty of Simón Bolívar and other Venezuelans to Ferdinand VII of Spain during their 1810 visit to London did not fool the British officials who received them. Many leading Britons, especially the merchants, hoped to capitalize on the confusion in Spain's colonies.

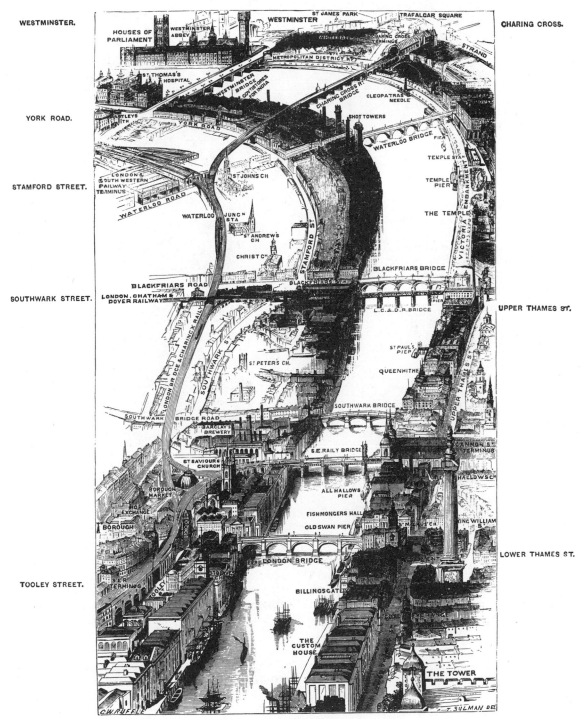

THE THAMES.
FROM THE TOWER TO WESTMINSTER.

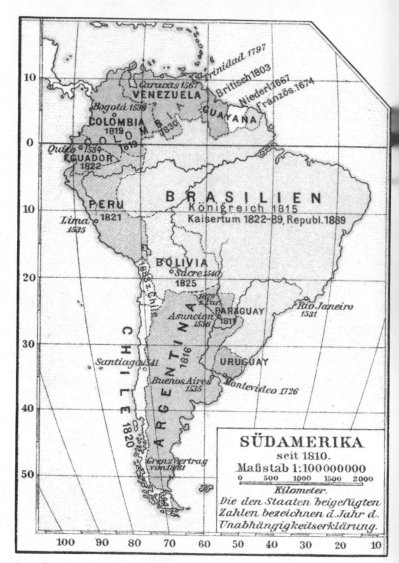

SÜDAMERIKA
seit 1810.
Maßstab 1:100000000
0   500   1000   1500   2000
Kilometer.
Die den Staaten beigefügten
Zahlen bezeichnen d. Jahr d.
Unabhängigkeitserklärung.

> *More than anyone, I desire to see America fashioned into the greatest nation in the world, greatest not so much by virtue of her area and wealth as by her freedom and glory.*
>
> —SIMÓN BOLÍVAR

South America in 1810. At this time most Spanish-American revolutionaries fully believed that the French occupation of Spain would prove permanent and that Ferdinand VII would never regain his throne.

it. The idea of independence for Venezuela had found its man in Bolívar.

"They say that great plans should be made with caution," he cried on July 3. "Are not three hundred years of caution enough? Do they want three hundred more?" His words swept away the last resistance. On July 4 the *junta* voted to do what the United States had done on that day 35 years before. The next day, by unanimous vote, they adopted a declaration of independence, and Venezuela became the first Spanish-American colony to be free.

Simón Bolívar in 1815.

> *You, Your Excellency, to whom America looks in victory, are the admiration and hope of your fellow-citizens. You are best fitted to unite the will of all the southern regions, to begin at once the creation of the great American nation, and to preserve it from the evils which have befallen the European system of nations.*
> —MUÑOZ TÉBAR
> Venezuelan secretary of state,
> in a letter to Bolívar,
> written in 1813

4

The Soldier

The revolution had carried the day, but Bolívar realized that that was not enough. It had been a peaceful revolution so far—all speeches and demonstrations and declarations—but now, he knew, it must be made real with blood.

The war began immediately, and Miranda accepted—after waiting 35 years for it!—the command of the Venezuelan army. He was a trained, experienced soldier, a veteran of countless campaigns on two continents, and he knew the science of war. What he did not know was the Venezuelans. He looked at the crowd of ragged farm workers hastily recruited to defend the new nation and haughtily demanded, "But where is my army?"

Spain moved swiftly to put down the colonial rebellion, and many royalist sympathizers in Venezuela rejected the new government. Miranda had all he could do to whip his untrained troops into shape and prepare them to meet the enemy which was everywhere. His manner did nothing to win their loyalty. He kept his old-fashioned uniform, his powdered hair, and his gold spurs, and openly showed his contempt for the raw recruits under him. After a day of abuse, his men deserted in droves.

Still, the old soldier had some success, and for a while it seemed victory was theirs. Although Bolívar

The empty tomb of Francisco Miranda in Caracas, Venezuela. Regarded as one of the great Spanish-American revolutionary generals, Miranda died in captivity in Spain in 1816. Once, while visiting the United States, he criticized the Massachusetts constitution, claiming that it gave "all the dignity...to property, which is the blight of such a democracy."

Simón Bolívar in 1820.

and Miranda had had a personal falling out—Miranda never trusted Bolívar's rich creole class and resented the younger man's interference in "his" army—they were united in their opposition to the Spanish.

But the situation was precarious. A Spanish naval officer, Juan Domingo Monteverde, arrived with a troop to oppose the revolutionaries and met with unexpected success. After winning a minor battle in the small town of Siquisiqui, Monteverde took over the Spanish army in Venezuela and seized the opportunity to advance against Miranda. He was a ruthless commander who encouraged his men to kill, rob, and burn whatever stood in their path. On March 23, 1812, he defeated another small body of Miranda's men. But then a different disaster fell.

On March 26 one of the worst earthquakes in history hit Caracas and other towns held by Venezuelan forces. It was Holy Thursday, and coincidentally the second anniversary of Emparán's expulsion, and many were in church. More than 10,000 people were killed in Caracas and La Guaira. Felipe Larrazábal, in his *Life of the Liberator Simon Bolivar*, quotes a survivor in Caracas:

"The churches, the buildings, all crumbled into pieces with awful din, burying all in their ruins. After that intolerable noise came the silence of death, broken only by the groans of the dying."

But the earthquake spared the royalist camps almost completely, and the religious saw it as a judgment of God, a divine punishment for the "treason" of the revolutionaries against their king.

Two 19th-century Peruvian Indians. Spanish *conquistadores*, under their famous leader Francisco Pizarro, took Peru in 1532, killing thousands of Indians, capturing their king, Atahualpa, and securing vast amounts of gold for shipment to Spain. Pizarro later founded the city of Lima as a base for further conquest and exploration.

Simón Bolívar and his colleagues discuss their plans following Venezuela's declaration of independence in 1811. Bolívar's brother Juan Vincente visited the United States that year to further the cause of Venezuelan independence. He proved more moderate than Simón, sending back not weapons but looms and machinery for printing money.

Priests, who believed in the "divine right of kings," were the group most loyal to the crown, and everywhere they spoke out against the revolution.

Bolívar, who narrowly escaped death during the earthquake, ran into the ruins to help the injured. A Spanish monarchist, José Díaz, who later described the scene in detail, saw him there and called out to him to admit that his cause was lost because even nature opposed it. But Bolívar was undaunted. He shouted his defiance—even nature would not stop the cause of liberty—and went on with his work.

A monk climbed onto the ruined altar of a fallen church and began a wild sermon against the new republic. Seeing Bolívar, he cursed him and cried out to the staring crowd to take God's vengeance on him.

Bolívar had to think and act fast; the crowd was growing ugly. If he stood his ground they would seize him, and if he tried to run away they would probably pursue and capture him. Muttering, the mob began to move in on him. There was only one thing to do. Drawing his sword, he strode through

> *In effect, nations move toward the pinnacle of their greatness in proportion to their educational progress. They advance if education advances; if it decays, they decay; and they are engulfed and lost in oblivion once education becomes corrupt or is completely abandoned.*
> —SIMÓN BOLÍVAR

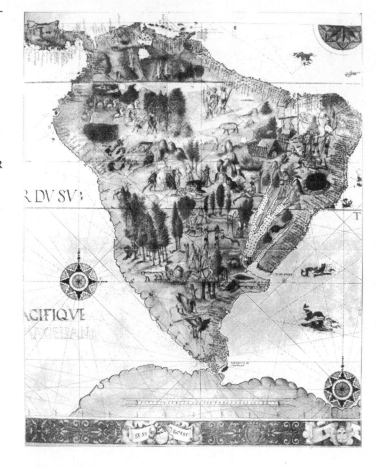

A 16th-century map of South America, demonstrating the extent to which colonization was still confined to the continent's coastal regions.

the sea of angry men and mounted the heap of rubble that had been an altar. Then with the flat of his sword he swept the crazed monk to the ground. The people of Caracas were stunned and slowly dispersed.

The troops were naturally discouraged, and so was Miranda; but Bolívar's spirit never flagged and seemed to sustain everyone else. The worst reverses never seemed to make Bolívar lose heart, the heaviest exertions never seemed to tire him. This frail little man—he was only 5' 6" tall and slim in build—was everywhere, doing the work of five men. No one could give up in the presence of such a leader.

No one, that is, except Miranda, whose dislike for Bolívar continued to grow. The brilliant young man was everything the grizzled old soldier was not—elegant, witty, inventive, and, above all, popular with the men—and it was no surprise that under the pressure of war they rubbed each other the wrong way. In the confusion following the earthquake, the governing council in Caracas had made Miranda commander-in-chief—virtually a military dictator of Venezuela—and he could give any order he wanted. So he sent Bolívar to command the fort at Puerto Cabello just to get him out of his hair.

It was a dangerous and difficult assignment, and Bolívar was not really equipped for it. On July 1 he wrote Miranda, "A traitor has seized the castle of San Felipe and is bombarding the town like a madman. If you do not attack at once, Puerto Cabello is lost."

Miranda hesitated. But he felt that the city could not be defended, so he did nothing. And Puerto Cabello fell. Bolívar and his staff barely escaped.

Miranda was more discouraged than ever. He had more soldiers than Monteverde but he did nothing with them. He might have attacked the weak Spanish army in Valencia or threatened them from the rear by attacking the royalist port at Coro where he had made his ill-fated attempt at an invasion six years before. But the old man had seemingly lost his nerve, and he spent all his time on drills. He clung to the old traditions of the European armies in which he had been trained and felt that if he could hound his men till they became a disciplined fighting force, all would yet be well. All this did was to drive more of his men to desert and give Monteverde time to regroup his army.

Monteverde pressed on ruthlessly, his troops growing with the deserters from Miranda's army. He flanked Miranda from the north and the south and forced him to retreat to Victoria, leaving behind a large store of food and ammunition. Miranda was at the end of his rope. "Venezuela is wounded to the heart," he said.

At last, on July 11, 1812 Miranda gave in. He sent a note to Monteverde offering to surrender. During the negotiations that followed, he slipped out of Victoria—leaving his men to fend for them-

Simón Bolívar displays the superb horsemanship which in 1819 gained him the approval of José Antonio Páez, the Venezuelan revolutionary leader who allied himself with Bolívar during the wars of independence. Páez eventually went on to lead a revolution against Bolívar in 1829.

British troops advance against the French in Spain in 1813, continuing the successful campaign which carried the fight to French soil later that year. Napoleon, who had squandered his forces in the Russian campaign of 1812, now found himself in retreat on all fronts.

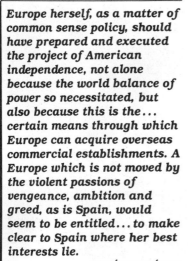

Europe herself, as a matter of common sense policy, should have prepared and executed the project of American independence, not alone because the world balance of power so necessitated, but also because this is the ... certain means through which Europe can acquire overseas commercial establishments. A Europe which is not moved by the violent passions of vengeance, ambition and greed, as is Spain, would seem to be entitled ... to make clear to Spain where her best interests lie.

—SIMÓN BOLÍVAR
in the *Jamaica Letter*,
written in 1815

selves—and went to La Guaira to arrange passage for himself to England. This was proof that he had really given up on the Republic of Venezuela and was looking out only for himself. There is also evidence that he accepted some money from the Spanish. The old adventurer, now 62, was not taking any chances.

When Bolívar heard of the surrender, he was furious and made straight for La Guaira. He and his men met Miranda the night before he was to sail.

They arrested the general for treason and handed him over to the commandant of La Guaira for safe-keeping until a court-martial could be convened to try him the next day. But the commandant had changed his loyalties and was now a royalist. To gain favor with the Spanish, the commandant turned Miranda over to Monteverde the next day. Under the terms of surrender which Miranda had set, Monteverde had no right to hold him, but the Spanish soldier, aware of how long and hard his government had tried to get their hands on this old man, clapped him in irons. Miranda never saw another day of freedom. He was transferred from dungeon to dungeon, from La Guaira to Puerto Rico to Spain. He spent the last four years of his life chained to the wall of a cell in Cadiz. When he died, his body was thrown into the mud, without even a name tag.

History has been kinder to Francisco de Miranda than his own times were. He is no longer seen as either a traitor or a coward, but as an unfortunate soldier who used outdated military methods, and was arrogant and, in the end, weak. He surrendered his 5,000 men to Monteverde's 4,000 and so signed away the fate of the First Republic of Venezuela. But no one now denies that he gave his life for the ideal of his country's independence; as Bolívar is known as the Liberator, Miranda has entered history as the Forerunner. Today, an empty marble coffin bearing his name stands near Bolívar's tomb in Caracas.

Venezuela was now in Monteverde's iron hand. He kept none of the promises he had made in accepting Miranda's surrender. He had promised there would be no reprisals, but once Miranda was safely in chains Monteverde rounded up and jailed all the patriots he could find. The leaders of the Venezuelan congress were sent to Spain in chains, and the constitution of the new country was publicly burned. A reign of terror began.

The gateway of the royal palace in Madrid. When Ferdinand VII returned to the Spanish throne in 1814, he persecuted many liberals who had fought for him against Napoleon. This served to warn the revolutionaries in Spanish America that he intended to fight for the restoration of the Spanish empire.

Simón Bolívar and Francisco Miranda attend the signing of Venezuela's independence declaration on July 5, 1811. British support for the Spanish-American separatist movements was diminishing rapidly at the time, reflecting disapproval of the abortive Mexican revolution of 1810, when thousands of Indians, led by a liberal priest, committed savage atrocities against the Spanish population.

The statue of Bolívar in Cartagena, Colombia.

Monteverde's men seized the property of all the leading creole citizens, and many were dragged off to prison on suspicion of being enemies of Spain. Bolívar got back to Caracas in disguise and hid out in the house of an old family friend, the Marqués de Casa León. He had to get out of the country before his role in the revolution became known. A Basque friend, Francisco Iturbe, who was also close to Monteverde, offered to help.

Monteverde knew Bolívar was a patriot, but not how influential he was. He agreed to issue him a passport "as a reward for the service he rendered the king by arresting the traitor Miranda."

During the audience with Monteverde Bolívar had been discreetly silent but at one point said, "I arrested Miranda for betraying his country, not to serve the King."

Monteverde hesitated, his pen poised over the document that would permit Bolívar to leave the country. "Don't pay any attention to him," Iturbe jumped in. "Give him the passport and let him go."

Monteverde was feeling good. He had everything he wanted now, and one more or one less hotheaded young man did not matter. He nodded to his friend and signed the paper. It was probably the worst mistake of his life.

The statue of Bolívar created by the famous French sculptor René Letourneur for the people of Ecuador.

5

The Liberator

The Simón Bolívar who slipped through the fingers of the Spanish in 1812 was a raw recruit, a rookie who had just begun to learn the art of war. Not yet 30 years old, he had seen his country become free and, after a year, fall back into the hands of Spain. He had seen a famous general fumble away victory, and he had experienced personal defeat at Puerto Cabello. He had learned something from it all, and he felt the time had come to fulfill his destiny. No longer a soldier in the army of an old general, Bolívar was ready to assume command. He was in flight from the Spanish, but his personal war with Spain had just begun.

He made for New Granada, a northwestern province covering present-day Panama, Colombia, and Ecuador. New Granada had begun to rebel around the same time as Venezuela, and some parts of it were already independent. Arriving at Cartagena, the principal port on the northwest coast, he offered his services to the independent government of the city.

He saw at once that New Granada was torn with conflicts. Cartagena and Bogotá, the present capital of Colombia, were rivals, and every independent city had its own government and its own ideas of politics.

As a visitor from another province, Bolívar didn't

Thomas Paine (1737-1809), the British-born radical who participated in both the American and French revolutions. The British government outlawed Paine in 1792 following the publication of *The Rights of Man*, in which he urged the British people to overthrow their monarchy.

Simón Bolívar c. 1810. Bolívar had returned to Venezuela from Europe in 1807, sailing aboard an American, rather than a Spanish, vessel. He thus avoided the possibility of confrontation with the navies of France and Britain, who were at war with Spain at the time.

A 17th-century drawing of Cartagena, the main port of the Spanish colony of New Granada. Simón Bolívar fled to Cartagena in 1812, following the reoccupation of Venezuela by forces loyal to the Spanish monarchy.

mix in Granadan internal affairs. He was already forming his own ideas, a great dream of a unified South America in which all provinces would be united into one country, like the United States to the north. He knew that New Granada could never be free if Venezuela was in the clutch of Spain, and that an army must be forged that would fight for freedom for both provinces at once.

He began to write for the local papers. His ringing words were the beginning of a political manifesto that would outline all the political philosophy of his career. Like Thomas Paine's 1776 pamphlet, *Common Sense*, its logic and eloquence persuaded many. In a series of open letters to the Granadans he analyzed his Venezuelan experience and called for a united attack on Spain under a strong central government. If the people of New Granada did not learn from Venezuela's mistakes, he warned, they too would suffer her fate.

The "Manifesto of Cartagena" was a great document, the first of Bolívar's powerful political statements. Profoundly reasoned, tightly logical, it ends on a note of passion:

"Let us hasten to break the chains of those who groan in the dungeons waiting for salvation from you. Do not betray their trust. Do not be deaf to the cries of your brothers. Avenge the dead, save the dying, relieve the oppressed, and bring freedom to all!"

The people were moved, and the government was impressed. They made him a colonel in their army and listened respectfully to his plan, outlined in his letters, to organize a force and march on Venezuela. It seemed a foolhardy idea—600 miles separated Cartagena from Caracas—but the congress was willing to consider it if Bolívar first demonstrated his ability.

He accepted a post in the small village of Barrancas on the Magdalena River. This river cut through royalist-held territory, and Spanish posts along it interfered with communications between Cartagena and Bogotá.

A 19th-century drawing of the Convent of St. Francis in Lima, Peru. José de San Martín's precarious liberation of the country in 1821 might have failed had it not been for the liberal revolt in Spain which had ousted Ferdinand VII a year earlier and thus deprived the royalist Peruvians of their political figurehead.

Bernardo O'Higgins (1778-1842), the soldier and statesman who took command of Chile's revolutionary forces in 1813. In collaboration with the Argentinian general José de San Martín, he crushed the Spaniards at Chacabuco on February 12, 1817, and ruled as dictator in Chile until 1823.

The captain who commanded Cartagena's army ordered Bolívar only to hold the fort, not to attack, but the young colonel saw an opportunity he could not resist. He organized 200 men and in rafts they floated upstream to the Spanish outpost at Tenerife. The surprise attack was so swift that the Spanish fled in confusion, leaving ships and ammunition behind.

Encouraged by this success, they pushed on to a village with the improbable name of Mompox, where 300 men joined his force. It was a turning point in his career. "I was born in Caracas," he said later, "but my fame was born in Mompox."

Nothing could stop him now. In December 1812 he won five victories in as many days, and in two weeks he cleared the river of Spanish royalists. Then he swept the valley along the Venezuelan border. In less than a month he overran all the enemy camps in the province of Santa Marta and was ready to march on Venezuela.

New Granada was convinced. It granted him honorary citizenship, promoted him to brigadier general, and gave him permission to launch the hardest and most dangerous campaign of his life. With a few hundred poorly equipped Granadans, he set out to conquer the vast land of Venezuela.

By now he had learned how to wage war, and this, along with his speed, daring, and imagination, allowed him to sweep away all before him. When his men were hopelessly outnumbered, he devised creative strategies to outwit the enemy. Once when a Spanish fort stood on a high hill before them, he sent a soldier with false attack plans into enemy territory, pretending to have lost his way. The man was captured and searched, and the Spanish confidently rushed off to trap Bolívar's troops at the location where an attack was supposedly planned. By the time the Spanish realized there was to be no attack there, Bolívar's men had already occupied the fort.

Bolívar was learning strategy, but it wasn't always easy; winning his battles with the enemy was sometimes easier than winning those with his own men. The enlisted men admired him and were inspired by his enthusiasm and his willingness to share their hardships, but the officers were often jealous and felt that he exceeded his authority. They resented being drawn into a war in a "foreign" province. They were Granadans. What was Venezuelan independence to them?

A Colonel Castillo finally resigned because, he said, invading Venezuela with Granadan troops was against his principles. His replacement, Francisco Santander, also refused to advance. This was too much for Bolívar; he realized that if such rebellion continued, it would undermine the discipline and morale of everybody. He drew his pistol on Santander and barked out "March! Either you and your men march at once or one of two things will happen: you will shoot me or, much more likely, I will shoot you."

Santander gave in, but he did not forget. It was the first of many confrontations between these two imperious men who were to serve together for fifteen years.

He had his problems, with men and with nature,

Mexico City's Grand Plaza around 1810. Mexico's revolutionary period began in 1810, when Miguel Hidalgo y Costilla, a liberal priest, called upon his Indian peasant parishioners to overthrow the government. His ragged army indiscriminately massacred thousands of Spaniards before royalist forces could organize and strike back.

Royalist infantry and cavalry patrol the streets of Lima, Peru, during the early 19th century.

but always Bolívar pressed on, taking town after town. From each he sent back a dispatch adding the word "libertada" (liberated) to the name of the city captured from the Spanish: Cúcuta libertada, Mérida libertada, Pamplona libertada, etc. In time he came to be known as El Libertador—the Liberator.

It was not a gentleman's war. Monteverde was ruthless and took no prisoners. He wiped out whole families of creoles merely suspected of sympathizing with the revolutionaries. Bolívar had no choice but to follow his example. All the rules of civilized warfare were suspended, and the country swam in a river of blood.

Venezuelan plainsmen and Spanish troops in 1813.

Bolívar's men covered the 600 miles to Caracas in 93 days, and arrived with 600 more men than he had when he first set out. Six thousand Spanish soldiers had fallen or fled before him and dozens of cities had been liberated. When, in August 1813, he marched triumphantly into his own city at the head of 800 patriots, he was officially given the title of Liberator—the title he always valued more than any other he was to receive.

Bolívar's triumph established him among the greatest military heroes in history, but it did not secure him in his position. While he tried frantically to restore order and establish a stable government in Caracas, trouble swirled all around him. Monteverde, who had fled to Puerto Cabello, was waiting for reinforcements from Spain to renew the battle. And back in New Granada jealous rival officers were complaining about Bolívar to the government. Worst of all, a new attack was being mounted against the capital from the plains.

The patriots held Monteverde in Puerto Cabello until 1,200 well-equipped Spanish troops arrived to rescue and support him. Even then the patriots fought so valiantly that they drove back the enemy. Monteverde took a musket ball through his jaw and was forced to give up his command.

Bolívar had to be everywhere and do everything at once. At the height of his glory he was under tremendous pressure, and issued the first of his many refusals to assume office. He had more urgent duties: the men of the plains were pressing forward and threatening the newly reestablished republic under a man even more dreadful than Monteverde.

José Tomás Boves was a Spaniard who had already had a colorful career as a smuggler. The confusion of war suited his talents exactly, and he soon made himself a leader among the half-savage plainsmen of Venezuela. His hatred of the patriot forces who had jailed him was unlimited. He was a fanatic, and he found the perfect following. The *llaneros*—men of the *llanos*, or plains—were descendents of frontiersmen and the Indians of the region—fierce, warlike, cannibalistic tribes which

A white explorer in South America, accompanied by Indian bearers, endures the rigors of the jungle during the early 19th century.

George Washington, first president of the United States (1789-1797), whose steady leadership gained him the title "Father of His Country." In 1824 Simón Bolívar's distinguished career earned him accolade as the George Washington of South America.

had never been fully civilized. Living with their horses on the land, they ate almost nothing but meat, either cooked over an open fire or made tender from long rides under the saddle and seasoned with the perspiration of their horses. Masterful horsemen, they could ride and fight for days without rest.

Boves offered these men unlimited loot and unlimited freedom—whatever they wanted from their victims. When they took a village, the women and the property were theirs; all Boves wanted for himself was the chance to kill the men and children. He enjoyed inventing barbarous tortures: tying men to trees, piercing their bodies with spears, and leaving them in the sun till thirst drove them mad; sending women the heads of their husbands and fathers; mutilating children in front of their parents. His favorite victims were creoles.

This madman—who didn't care for alcohol, tobacco, or women—struck terror in everyone in his path, and his following of *llaneros* and fugitives grew to a mighty force. The royalists were quick to exploit it by encouraging Boves, and his horde became a sort of unofficial—but deadly—Spanish army. Even the royalists found it frightening. They called it "the Legion of Hell." Boves was not inappropriately known as "the Beast."

Although Bolívar insisted that he wanted no office,

Antonio José Sucre, the brilliant general who led Bolívar's forces to victory over the Spanish in Peru at the Battle of Ayacucho on December 9, 1824.

Delegates attend the Philadelphia Convention of 1787, at which James Madison (who was eventually to meet Bolívar's brother in 1811) gained his reputation as a great constitutionalist. While Bolívar admired the American political system, he never considered it an ideal model upon which to base a liberal government in South America.

Miguel Hidalgo y Costilla (1753–1811), the radical priest who led the peasant revolt against the Spanish government in Mexico in 1810. A brilliant scholar, Hidalgo gained his radical convictions during his serious reading of Rousseau and other liberals.

no other responsibility, than that of leading his men into battle, he accepted the role of dictator. Historians have questioned his sincerity in always refusing office and then giving in and accepting it, but there seems little doubt that this time the honor was unwelcome. He knew the need for an authoritative government in the chaotic city he had just liberated, but he sincerely disliked supreme authority. Even his experience as a military commander had not altered his democratic philosophy. "Flee from that country where one man holds all the power," he stated at this time. "It is a land of slaves."

He consented, however, to reestablish order and set up a constitution for the new republic. He worked tirelessly, but he knew that one man could not run a government and hold off the enemy in the field at the same time. And the enemy was all around them.

Monteverde's successor had 4,000 men at Puerto

Emperor Napoleon I of France and his wife, Empress Josephine, receive homage from their courtiers in December 1804.

78

General José de San Martín, the Protector of Peru. San Martín's suggestion that only the importation of a European prince could secure the political stability of Peru found no favor with Bolívar when the two men met at Guayaquil in July 1822.

Cabello, with more arriving every week. Another Spanish army with 3,000 was moving in from the east. And Boves, with 8,000 fierce horsemen, was pressing ever closer to Caracas from the south.

The republic might still have been saved if there had been the one thing Bolívar had called for from the beginning: unity. But Bolívar's generals would never pull together. Jealous and ambitious, they fought among themselves and with Bolívar. Santander still refused to cooperate with a Venezuelan and would not recognize Bolívar's authority; General Mariño, the commander in the eastern provinces, also refused to come to the rescue of Caracas.

Finally Bolívar realized that he had no choice but to lead his army, along with some 30,000 civilian refugees, out of the city. Almost no one remained but a few monks, some nuns, and the old and sick who preferred to meet death in their own homes.

Bolívar joined Mariño in the east, since Mariño would not come to him, but even together their armies were no match for Boves's savage cavalry. In

Bernardo O'Higgins, the soldier and statesman who freed Chile from Spanish rule in 1817 and ruled the country until 1823, when conservative opponents of his progressive reforms exiled him to Peru.

the city they might have stood off the horsemen, but in the field they were shattered. At the battle of La Puerta on June 15, 1814, the plainsmen under Boves destroyed the combined armies of Bolívar and Mariño, and the second republic died. It had had an even shorter life than the first.

Boves continued his triumphal sweep through the fallen land, killing all whites he encountered. His name elicited so much fear that cities surrendered at the first sign of his approach. The 14-year-old sister of Marshal Sucre threw herself off a balcony rather than fall into his hands. Boves occupied Caracas in July, and his atrocities finally led his commanding officer to complain of him to Spain. "He is turning the country into a desert," he reported. Madrid's reply was that the government approved of Boves's conduct with a vote of thanks for his valuable service.

However, 1814 was to see the last victory of Tomás Boves. His black flag bordered with skulls fell in the bloody battle of Urica in December when he defeated General Ribas, Bolívar's long-time friend. Ribas was betrayed after the battle by a slave his army had freed. The Spanish cut off Ribas's head, fried it in oil to preserve it, and displayed it on a spike in the main plaza of Caracas. That was how the Spanish waged war.

Boves did not live to enjoy the spectacle. A young black soldier ran him through with a *llanero* lance during the battle, and Venezuela breathed a sigh of relief. "He was not nourished with mother's milk," Bolívar wrote later, "but with the blood of tigers."

In the meantime, Bolívar had returned to New Granada in September, in exile for the second time in two years. Despite the failure of his mission, despite the loss of the cream of Granadan youth, the government recognized his heroism. He was received warmly and appointed commander-in-chief.

But he had enemies in New Granada, too. There were accusations. They said he had abandoned his troops, and that he wanted to make himself a dictator in New Granada as he had in Venezuela.

Ambition for power and glory was always too close to the surface of Bolívar's mind to be denied completely, and there was perhaps enough truth in the accusation to hurt. Regardless, he did not want to be a cause of controversy in his new home, so he resigned his command and set out for Jamaica.

Napoleon Bonaparte's body, dressed in the uniform of a marshal of France, lies in state on May 7, 1821, two days after his death. Napoleon died on St. Helena, the British island in the southern Atlantic where he spent his last years in exile.

A street scene in Buenos Aires, Argentina, around 1805. Following Argentina's independence declaration in 1810, the new republic's top military men realized that their continued independence required the destruction of Spain's armies in Chile and Peru.

Maybe the English there would give him the support he needed.

Napoleon had fallen in April 1814 and Ferdinand—the long-awaited hope of the conservatives—had been put back on the throne of Spain. The world waited to see how he would deal with the colonies. The supporters who had restored him to power had received promises of a more liberal policy and greater freedom for South America. The day Bolívar sailed for Jamaica, June 9, 1815, Ferdinand VII signed a decree promising an end to the troubles in the colonies.

He meant it, too, but not in the way it sounded. He meant to crush any remaining spark of rebellion in the New World, and demanded unconditional surrender and submission from all its leaders. When there was opposition of the mildest sort, he responded with the strongest force. He had already dispatched an army of 15,000 of his best men under his most experienced general to put down any and all uprisings that remained. They had orders to be merciless, in the great Spanish tradition.

At this time, only two or three areas of South America had any significant revolutionary activity. José de San Martín, the Liberator of Argentina, was keeping the spirit alive in the province then known as Río de la Plata. Bernardo O'Higgins was organizing a republic in Chile. And then, of course, there was Bolívar. Spanish General Pablo Morillo set out to finish off any revolutionary movement in Cartagena and Venezuela, and then to move southward to put an end to San Martín.

In a way, Ferdinand's policy of war to the death did the cause of independence in South America more good than a liberal policy might have. His measures were so harsh, his punishments so severe, that he turned everyone against him. Creoles who had supported the Spanish and opposed the revolution were rounded up indiscriminately with the rest. The worst excesses of Monteverde were repeated: whole city councils were hanged publicly; families were executed without trial; the colonies were stripped of the few liberties they had. Finally his

A view of 19th-century Jamaica, the British island in the Caribbean where in 1815 Bolívar spent seven months, following the fall of the Second Venezuelan Republic in 1814.

Port Antonio, Jamaica, during the early 19th century. By 1815 (when Bolívar visited Jamaica) Ferdinand VII had declared his intention to crush the separatists throughout Spanish America. His decision constituted a rejection of the mediation attempts which the British had been making since 1811.

strongest supporters turned against him.

Historians agree that Ferdinand did as much to stir up revolution in his colonies as the revolutionaries did. As Samuel Eliot Morison wrote in his *History of the American People*, "Ferdinand VII, the monarch restored in 1814, was such an imbecile that the colonies had to strike for freedom."

In Jamaica, Bolívar saw the new resolve of his people. Yet recognizing the danger that the fallen Napoleon might try to get a foothold in the New World, he devoted himself to writing and trying to create sympathy for his cause. His famous "Jamaica Letter" of 1815 analyzes the problems of South America and lays the blame, as always, on a lack of unity. The essay is written with such clarity and insight into the situation that it could have been composed today, with the advantage of hindsight.

The "Jamaica Letter" anticipates much that has

been written and done during the nearly two centuries since it was composed. As always, Bolívar seeks a union of all South American nations—like the Organization of American States that, many years later, finally did come into being.

Even in defeat, Bolívar was confident of the destiny of the continent. Wherever he went, after liberating a city he established a democratic, representative congress in it before pushing on—in preparation for the day he was sure was coming when the country and the continent would be free and at peace. And now, at the lowest point in his fortunes, he confidently called for a meeting in Panama to discuss a unified solution to the problems of the continent.

But no one was listening. As usual, the English did not want to offend anyone else by getting involved with colonial problems. And while the English ignored him, his own people were actively plotting against him. One night when he gave his own bed to a visitor, a stranger crept in and put a knife into the unfortunate guest. It was one of many times in Bolívar's life when he had narrowly escaped death. It convinced him that he had an important destiny. It also convinced him that it was time to get out of Jamaica.

And he got out just in time. He left in May 1815, and in July Morillo's troops began a bitter siege of Cartagena. For 100 days the brave patriots held out, until no hope remained. Historian John Lynch, in *Spanish American Revolutions*, gives a dramatic account: "Cartagena maintained a suicidal resistance, its streets and houses littered with corpses, and the few patriots still alive were butchered by the royalists."

The Spanish finished the job of "pacification," as they called it, by crushing Bogotá in May 1816. The royalist leader Juan Sámano kept up the Spanish standard of cruelty by having all the leading citizens publicly executed—some were hanged, some shot, some beheaded—and confiscating all the property. Workers were all forced into labor gangs. New Granada was a slave camp. There was no going back for Bolívar now.

Alexandre Pétion (1770-1818), president of the black republic of Haiti (formerly the French colony of Saint Domingue) from 1807 to 1818. Pétion's generosity to Bolívar and other Spanish-American refugees stemmed from his liberal views, which he also put to use in supporting the slave rebellion which secured Haiti's independence from France in 1804.

Jean-Jacques Dessalines (1758-1806), emperor of Haiti from 1804 to 1806. Born a slave, in 1797 he joined the black rebels under Toussaint L'Ouverture. Following the expulsion of the French after several years of fighting, Dessalines established the Haitian republic in 1804.

In 1815 there were just two free countries in the New World: the United States, which had always ignored Bolívar's call for help, and Haiti. This tiny all-black republic was a natural choice for the Liberator. Its president, Alexandre Pétion, gave him full support—ships, arms, money, even men. In return, Bolívar promised the ex-slave Pétion something he had always promised for Venezuela—to abolish slavery. He had freed his own slaves the year before. Now he meant to make it a law.

The first expedition against Venezuela failed for the usual reasons—lack of support from an indifferent Venezuelan population and arguments among Bolívar's own officers. But Bolívar never gave up. Before the end of 1816 he was at it again. And this time he got a foothold.

Bolívar's men continued to follow him without question, but his staff still argued among themselves and disobeyed his orders. Bolívar's patience was a marvel: he wrote his officers flattering memos praising their service; he promoted them; he let them have their way when he could. But nothing helped.

The breaking point came with Manuel Piar, a mulatto general. Piar had shown wonderful courage and skill in the eastern campaign, but he had openly ignored Bolívar's orders not to execute prisoners, and he was sent back to Haiti. Piar refused to go. Instead, he deserted and started a rebellion against Bolívar among his fellow mulattos. It was a showdown, and Bolívar could not risk a race war within his own ranks. He brought Piar up before a court-martial, which sentenced him to death for treason. It was a painful decision for Bolívar, but it showed everyone who was in charge.

He progressed slowly toward Caracas. One by one the Spanish posts in the east fell before his men. As he advanced, he continued to set up orderly governments.

When he reached the small town of Angostura—now Ciudad Bolívar (Bolívar City)—on the Orinoco River, he decided that the time had come to establish a national government, even if he didn't really have a nation yet. He knew that the rest of the world would never believe in the Republic of Venezuela if it had nothing to show but a series of guerrilla victories. He needed a real government, a set of laws, and a constitution guaranteeing the rights of its citizens.

In February 1819 he called the Congress of Angostura. It was gathered together with little preparation. Bolívar delivered a speech outlining his ideas of political organization and presented a constitution for the Congress to vote on. It was much like that of the United States and included distribution of land, reasonable taxation, and a representative government. But it was not what we would consider completely democratic. It called for a life term for the president, for example, and a

Toussaint L'Ouverture (1743-1803), the Haitian independence leader. A republican in the tradition of the leaders of the French Revolution, L'Ouverture was imprisoned in France in 1802 for resisting the expedition sent by Napoleon to restore slavery in Saint-Domingue, which became independent Haiti in 1804.

senate whose members passed their positions on to their children, like the British House of Lords. Bolívar did not believe his people were ready for complete democracy yet, and he felt they had to be realistic about what would work.

His most strongly urged recommendation was for the removal of "the dark mantle of barbarous and profane slavery." He argued passionately that the institution of slavery contradicted everything the revolution stood for. Thus he kept faith with President Pétion of Haiti, and with his own conscience. Unfortunately, the rich were not ready to give up their valuable human property. Although the Congress of Angostura voted in favor of freeing the slaves, full national emancipation did not occur in Venezuela until 1854, 24 years after the Liberator's death. Still, Venezuela freed its slaves nine years before Lincoln's Emancipation Proclamation accomplished the same thing for the United States.

The new government had nothing to govern. It was similar to a government in exile, representing

Simón Bolívar addresses the Congress of Angostura on February 18, 1819. Bolívar's speech showed his increasing fear that democracy might never work in South America.

A Spanish-American plantation owner gives orders to his slaves. Bolívar's passionate attack on slavery during his speech at Angostura in 1819 failed to secure immediate emancipation for Venezuela's slaves. The propertied classes had no wish to lose the cheap labor which contributed to their prosperity.

a country that had not yet fully come into being. Yet they voted a constitution into effect—approving most of Bolívar's suggestions except for that of a hereditary senate—and they elected Bolívar president. He accepted the post on condition that he could go on with the war. In less than two weeks after his election, he turned the government over to his vice-president and was off once more to the front.

His first step was to join the legendary José Antonio Páez, who had won the plainsmen over to the patriot side when Boves fell. A *llanero* himself, Páez was the only man who could control these fierce plainsmen. He had been "born in the saddle," and his men boasted that he was half horse. He set such an example of reckless courage that they followed him, like children. As bloodthirsty as his men, Páez had a genius for guerrilla warfare, and he molded the *llaneros* into a disciplined fighting force. Instead of plunder, he offered them something better—a share of the estates confiscated from the enemy. A savage fighter and a brilliant tactician, he was loyal to Bolívar, but he was not a man to be commanded. He would not fight outside of his beloved plains. Páez was a king in his own country. Nobody could give him orders.

Bolívar won his loyalty almost by accident. When

All our moral powers will not suffice to save our infant republic from this chaos unless we fuse the mass of the people, the government, the legislation, and the national spirit into a single united body. Unity, unity, unity must be our motto in all things. The blood of our citizens is varied: let it be mixed for the sake of unity. Our Constitution has divided the powers of government: let them be bound together to secure unity.
—SIMÓN BOLÍVAR
speaking at the Congress of Angostura in 1819

A 19th-century artist's impression of an encounter between Spanish-American settlers and members of the native Indian population. The painting reflects the romantic view of pioneer existence taken by many 19th-century artists.

José Antonio Páez (1790-1873), the Venezuelan plainsman who allied himself and his followers with Bolívar in 1819. An able general, Páez emerged during the 1820s as an unscrupulous and dictatorial politician, leading the revolt against Bolívar in 1829.

the plainsman saw how Bolívar handled his horse, he knew this was a man beside whom he could fight and thus he pledged his support.

Together they decided that the first order of business had to be to return to New Granada and relieve General Santander, who was about to be overwhelmed by Morillo's forces. It seemed an impossible expedition, and nobody but Páez and Bolívar could have accomplished it. They marched, rode, swam, and waded through the worst conditions, across mountains, plains, and swamps, through rivers and lakes. "For seven days," Bolívar's aide O'Leary reported, "we marched in water up to our waists." They rarely slept. They passed through areas swollen with rains and staggered across Andean passes 12,000 feet high.

They improvised bridges and swam cattle and horses across streams swarming with alligators and man-eating fish. Some men died of tropical fever and others froze in the snow of the Andes. In all, the army lost more than a quarter of its men and horses on the march. The expedition has been compared with that of Hannibal crossing the Alps to invade Rome, but the Carthaginian had nothing as bad as the "green hell" of Venezuela to face.

Yet everywhere they won. The Spanish, fresh, well-equipped, outnumbering the ragged little band of patriots, fell before them in battle after battle. At last in August 1819 the Battle of Boyacá turned the tide and the Spanish lost heart.

When the troops got to Bogotá, they found it deserted. The royalists had fled. Sámano, knowing the revenge he could expect from the patriots for his reign of terror, ran out disguised as an Indian. He was in such a hurry that he left the city's entire treasury on his desk.

Bolívar had food and money now, so he could relax. But there was still work to be done, and he never stopped. He set up a provisional government. He was already president, but he had higher am-

Abraham Lincoln (1809-1865), the American president who paved the way for the abolition of slavery in the United States in 1863, 44 years after Bolívar had called for the emancipation of Venezuela's slaves in a speech at Angostura.

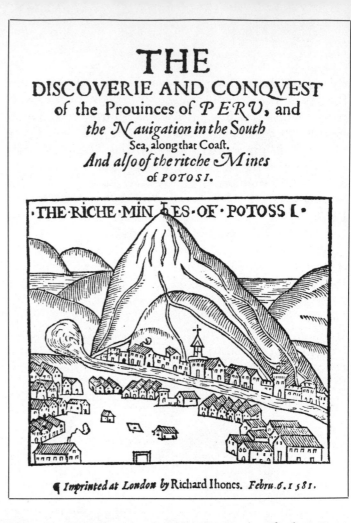

THE
DISCOVERIE AND CONQVEST
of the Prouinces of *PERV,* and
the *Nauigation in the South*
Sea, along that Coast.
And also of the ritche *Mines*
of *POTOSI.*

·THE·RICHE·MIN ES·OF·POTOSS I·

Imprinted at London by Richard Ihones. *Febru.6.1581.*

The title page of a 16th-century book concerning the Spanish discovery and conquest of Peru. One of the great original bases for Spanish colonial expansion in South America, Peru remained staunchly royalist until republican forces under Antonio José Sucre destroyed the Spanish armies in Peru at Ayacucho on December 9, 1824.

bitions. His dream had always been a unified nation, and he declared the Republic of *Gran Colombia*—Greater Colombia—including both New Granada and Venezuela, an area of nearly a million square miles. He created the post of vice-president for New Granada and assigned it to Santander.

Francisco de Paula Santander was a good, if dangerous, choice. A born administrator from a creole family as established as Bolívar's, he had been trained as a lawyer. In the field, his men had found him cold and remote, and they often refused to obey him. But in office, the 27-year-old Santander knew exactly what he wanted and how to get things done. Unfortunately, what he wanted was often different from what Bolívar wanted. He was as ambitious as his commander, and the two were to clash often, as they had before.

Bolívar knew there was trouble ahead, not from the Spanish—he could handle them—but from his own ambitious officers. He was often discouraged. "Wherever I go," he wrote in a letter in 1819, "there is disunity and disintegration. Soon it will be death. What devilish people we have here!"

By 1820 Bolívar's victories persuaded Spain to negotiate, and he and Morillo met in November. Bolívar wore his usual blue army fatigues as he rode up to the splendidly uniformed Spanish general. "That little man in the blue coat sitting on a mule—*that* is Bolívar?" Morillo was heard to exclaim.

The two embraced in Spanish fashion, and talked and drank toasts together all through the night. Bolívar said later that he deliberately pretended to be friendly and frank; if so, he succeeded, because Morillo was very impressed, and eagerly signed a six-month truce. This was just what Bolívar wanted.

The Inca ruins at Machu Picchu in Peru. It was in this harsh and desolate landscape that Bolívar's army fought the inconclusive Battle of Junín in 1824.

French troops commanded by General Rochambeau drown mulatto and black slaves in Le Cap Bay, Saint-Domingue, in 1803. The savage action taken by the French against the slaves of Saint-Domingue failed to regain the colony, which became Haiti in 1804.

It gave his army time to regroup and it showed the world that Spain took the new republic seriously, rather than as a pack of rebels.

The truce did not last for six months, however. Soon the war resumed and Morillo, a sympathetic and just man, asked to be relieved and went home to Spain.

His replacement was unprepared for command, and his soldiers were demoralized by their long run of defeats. On June 21, 1821, the combined forces of Mariño, Páez, and Bolívar converged on the main body of the Spanish army in Venezuela at Carabobo. This final battle was brief and decisive. Spain was at last defeated in Venezuela. Eight days later Bolívar once more entered Caracas in triumph.

Again he was made president and again he left, this time putting Páez in charge. He did it with misgivings, knowing how undependable the greedy, nearly illiterate *llanero* chieftain was, but he felt he had to be tactful to keep his loyalty. With the cunning and ambitious Santander representing him in Bogotá, and the simple, easily influenced Páez in Caracas, Bolívar was very nervous. Everything he had won in war seemed likely to be lost in victory.

He could have stayed to govern his newly created nation of Colombia himself, of course, but he declared that an office had become "a torment" to him. He felt he had a more important job—to conquer the province of Quito (modern Ecuador) and add it to his republic.

General Antonio José de Sucre was his choice to lead the invasion. Thirteen years younger than Bolívar, Sucre was his favorite—the man he would have chosen to be his son, he said. Sucre had been trained as an engineer, and brought the calm, resolute mind of a professional to the job of war. "Sucre is in all things a nobleman," Bolívar wrote. "He has the best-organized mind in Colombia. He is the best general of the Republic and its first statesman. He is the bravest of the brave and the truest of the true." Together in May 1822 they won the battle of Bombóná and added Quito to the republic.

Bolívar was satisfied. He wanted to go home, be

with his family, and relax. But two months after Bombóná he received a visit which changed the course of his life and the history of South America.

His visitor was José de San Martín, "the best soldier in South America." The liberator of Argentina, the hero of Chile, San Martín was the only man the Spanish feared and respected as much as they did Bolívar. He had done in the south what Bolívar had done in the north, and sooner or later their paths were bound to meet. Now, in the port city of Guayaquil, the Argentine general asked Bolívar for help.

San Martín had advanced northward as far as Lima, Peru, but could make no further headway. Peru was the last and strongest royalist domain, the only remaining outpost of Spain's power on the continent. With Bolívar's help, San Martín might sweep out the last of the Spanish.

The details of this famous meeting can never be known because it was held in private. The two men were opposite in many ways, and it was unlikely that they would agree. San Martín was a professional soldier trained by the Spanish, for whom he

> *Venezuela, on breaking away from Spain, has recovered her independence, her freedom, her equality, and her national sovereignty. By establishing a democratic republic, she has proscribed monarchy, distinctions, nobility, prerogatives and privileges. She has declared for the rights of man and freedom of action, thought, speech, and press.*
> —SIMÓN BOLÍVAR
> speaking at the Congress of Angostura in 1819

The shrine at Le Cap in Haiti, erected by victorious rebel slaves to commemorate their hard-won independence from France. Under the leadership of President Pétion, the Haitian government showed Simón Bolívar great hospitality in 1815, and financed his return to Venezuela.

Simón Bolívar's cavalry charge the Spanish at the Battle of Carabobo, June 24, 1821. The battle might have gone against Bolívar's forces but for the bravery of his British contingent. The British drew the Spaniards' fire until the rest of Bolívar's men were properly prepared for action and ready to advance.

had fought loyally for 20 years before becoming a revolutionary. He was a profound royalist in philosophy. He wanted to free South America from Spain and then find another royal family in Europe to govern it.

Bolívar did not want a king to rule Colombia or any other part of South America. He refused to help. He would neither send troops, nor would he command. San Martín was very disappointed. The tough, practical general found Bolívar superficial, impractical, and vain—a man with a passion for power who refused to share the glory of liberation. He knew he could neither compete nor serve with him, so he retired to France. At 44, his career had come to an end, and for the remaining 28 years of his life the proud old soldier never spoke of the meeting.

For a year Bolívar sat tight, enjoyed a scandalous love affair, and tried to keep his country together. He recognized Peru as a neighbor and tried to help her in her struggles by sending troops, as San Martín had requested, but the Spanish were too

José Antonio Páez, one of Bolívar's most gifted generals, calls upon his fleeing horsemen to turn and face the Spanish during the New Granada campaign of 1819. Bolívar's army suffered several defeats in this campaign before gaining a decisive victory at Boyacá on August 7, 1819.

A 19th-century lithograph of Lima in Peru, where in 1825 Bolívar devised a constitution for the new republic of Bolivia (previously known as Upper Peru).

Simón Bolívar and Argentinian general José de San Martín meet at Guayaquil on July 26, 1822. The two men failed to reach agreement on San Martín's request for military assistance for his Peruvian campaign, and the Argentinian left Guayaquil early on July 28, leaving the ball Bolívar had given for him without a word of farewell.

much for the revolutionaries. Spain controlled the highlands and so controlled the country. San Martín had declared Peru free three years before, but after his resignation it had relapsed into anarchy. Peru needed a Bolívar, and he knew he had to go.

His Colombian congress, however, did not want its president wasting money and lives in a foreign war. Few shared his dream of union. But his powers of persuasion had not deserted him, and he finally got their approval for this last expedition against the Spanish.

With an army of 9,000—the largest he ever had—he set out for Peru in 1823. In August 1824 he scattered the Spanish at Junín.

On December 9, 1824 his faithful general Sucre did the same at Ayacucho. He brilliantly outmaneuvered and defeated the last major Spanish force in South America. Peru, "the reluctant republic," was free. It was the last important battle in the wars of independence in the New World.

6

The Exile

The Liberator of Venezuela renounces forever and declines unequivocally to accept any office except at the head of our soldiers in defense of the salvation of our country.
—SIMÓN BOLÍVAR
in a proclamation issued in Caracas in 1813

Simón Bolívar had fulfilled his dream as few people in history have done. He had pulled the most precious jewel out of the crown of Spain and freed half a continent. The world was at his feet. Colombia called him President and Peru called him Dictator. In 1825 High Peru, a southeastern province of Peru claimed by both Peru and Argentina, was declared independent and assumed the name Bolívar, later changed to Bolivia. It too named him President—for life.

Glory and money and power showered over him. George Washington's family sent a gold medal once belonging to the United States president to "the Second Washington of the New World." He was offered the title of Emperor of the Andes, and back in Caracas Páez seriously urged him to become Simón I, King of Venezuela.

He resisted the temptations but he thoroughly enjoyed the attention. It was the high point of his life. If he had retired then, as he always said he would, he might have lived out his years honored and loved.

But the need for power and glory is a hard habit to break. And Bolívar still had a dream—a federation of the Andes, including all the Spanish-speaking republics of South America. It was a great ideal, but he was to find it a lot harder to win the

George Washington, president of the United States from 1789 to 1797. In 1825 Washington's family sent Bolívar a medal which had once belonged to the great American revolutionary and constitutionalist.

Simón Bolívar in 1823, the year in which Ferdinand VII, with French assistance, regained the Spanish throne and repealed the liberal reforms enacted by the constitutionalists who had seized power in 1820.

101

Agustín de Iturbide (1783-1824), the creole adventurer who negotiated Mexico's independence from Spain in 1821.

peace than it had been to win the war.

Bolívar had always had faith in his dream. Even before the Battle of Ayacucho in 1824 he was so sure of success that he began to organize a meeting of free governments to be held in Panama. It was to be the beginning of a Spanish-American League of Nations. He had given up the idea of complete union—a single nation covering the continent—but he foresaw a close federation of independent nations. To get the world to take the meeting seriously, he invited England and the United States.

He saw the conference in grandiose terms—not very realistic, perhaps, but glorious. Its first day would be "immortal in American history," he said in a circular that he sent to the invited governments. It would create a new age of international harmony and peace—everyone working together in mutual cooperation and love.

In fact, whether or not the rest of the world took the congress of Panama seriously, most of its own intended members did not. When it finally met in 1826, it was, in historian Harold Blakemore's words, "a dismal failure." The United States delegate fell ill and could not attend, the English delegate refused to participate, and most of the Latin-American countries either sent their regrets or ignored their invitations. Only Mexico, Guatemala, Colombia, and Peru took part.

The delegates agreed in principle to a treaty of mutual help and protection but could not guarantee their governments' agreement. And the union, even if approved by its four members' governments, would have little strength. The whole affair was a great disappointment to Bolívar, who had entertained such big hopes.

History has seen it in a better light—as a forerunner and model of international organizations to come. Sixty-four years later, in 1890, the Pan-American Union took its inspiration from Bolívar's ill-fated congress of Panama, and today's Organization of American States is its direct descendant.

The failure of his dream of a League of Nations however, was one of the least of his disappointments at this time. Everywhere around him the fruits of his victories were slipping away. In Lima his time was spent trying to keep peace between Peru and its neighbors, and only his own prestige kept it from war. "Although Bolívar is extremely popular . . . in Peru, still there is such a jealousy, if not hatred, between Peruvians and Colombians there can be no real cordiality between the two peoples," wrote an English observer in 1825.

Worse yet, unbearable tensions were beginning to be felt in Colombia itself. Santander in Bogotá ordered military conscription, and Páez in Caracas refused. Both were furious and wanted to break apart. Quito, the third part of Gran Colombia, was threatening to secede too. Bolívar, with a sigh, hurried back to try to patch things up.

Páez, the old plainsman, had made himself immensely wealthy. He was a virtual dictator in Venezuela, and although with tears in his eyes he swore loyalty to Bolívar, he continued to do as he pleased. Bolívar's embraces and compliments only postponed the inevitable in Caracas.

In Bogotá it was clear that Santander wanted none of Bolívar. He was in charge and resented the interference of this "supreme disturber of the Republic," as he called him in a letter to a friend.

On the night of September 25, 1828, Bolívar once again narrowly escaped assassination. He was sleeping when a group of conspirators—supported, if not organized, by Santander—broke into his chamber crying "Death to the tyrant! *Viva* Santander!" Only the quick thinking of his mistress, Manuela Sáenz, won him time to escape. While she stalled the assassins, the Liberator jumped nine feet to the ground and hid in a ditch.

This was the last straw for Bolívar. He had escaped the daggers of steel, but he would never recover from the emotional pain. He took charge again, exiled Santander (he wanted to have him executed, like Piar, but could not risk creating a martyr and starting a civil war), and left for Quito.

But it was too late. Greater Colombia, and indeed all of Spanish America, was falling apart faster than he could put it back together. The state of

Lord George Canning (1770-1827), the British foreign secretary who in 1823 recognized the independence of the South American republics in revolt against Spain.

A Spanish *conquistador* of the 16th century. The *conquistadores*, pioneers of Spanish expansion into South America, displayed great strength and courage which seem to have been passed down through the generations, judging by the epic military feats of men like Bolívar during the early 19th century.

Dom Pedro I, emperor of Brazil from 1822 to 1831. Bolívar expressed interest in liberating Brazil from Portugal in 1825, but failed to gain support for his plan from the other South American republics.

things was best described by Bolívar himself in a despairing letter written in 1829:

"America is in chaos. Peru is on the verge of upheaval. Bolivia has had three presidents in five days, and two of them have been murdered. In Buenos Aires they have overthrown the president. Mexico has been convulsed by violent revolution."

Everywhere Bolívar's dream of freedom and unity lay in ruins about him. It seemed, after all, that his enemies had been right—Latin America needed a king because it could not govern itself. In 1830 Venezuela and Quito seceded, leaving only New Granada with the name Colombia. South America had apparently won its war only to lose its peace, its prosperity, and its happiness.

The new government feared Bolívar's interference. Venezuela ordered him out of the country. Having sold most of his property to pay the troops, he was almost penniless now, and had to write his sister to sell the last piece of land to provide him with traveling money. In June of 1830, to top everything off, he learned that Marshal Sucre, his closest friend and political heir, had been murdered.

Broken in health—his physical condition had been deteriorating for the past year—the Liberator painfully made his way into Colombia, hoping to return to Europe, unable to live in "a country where the noblest patriots are foully murdered." His disillusion and despair were complete. In November he told a friend: "America is ungovernable. Those who fight in her revolution plough the sea. The only thing to do in America is emigrate."

A month later, on December 17, 1830, tuberculosis claimed the frail little body of the 47-year-old Liberator of South America.

Simón Bolívar saw his life as a failure. Everything he had worked for had disappeared before his eyes. At the end he compared himself with his

I have held power for twenty years, and I have drawn but a few sure conclusions. 1. America is ungovernable for us. 2. He who serves a revolution plows the sea. 3. The only thing one can do in America is to emigrate. 4. This country will infallibly fall into the hands of an unbridled crowd of petty tyrants almost too small for notice and of all colors and races. 5. Devoured by all the crimes and extinguished by ferocity, we shall be disdained by the Europeans. 6. If it were possible for a part of the world to fall back to primitive chaos, America would.
—SIMÓN BOLÍVAR
shortly before his death

A statue of Simón Bolívar in Caracas, Venezuela.

Simón Bolívar's tomb in Caracas, Venezuela.

old favorite Don Quixote—a madman who had made himself ridiculous trying to right the world's wrong.

But history has judged him very differently. A man who had a deeper perception of his times than had his contemporaries, a visionary who saw the moral needs of his country, and a man of action who moved decisively to achieve them—if he failed to bring about his dream, he planted and nourished the seed of it with his life. Only now, a century and a half after his death, is the goodly tree of liberty, peace, and justice beginning to flourish. The life of Simón Bolívar, dedicated and sacrificed to its growth, was not spent in vain.

Chronology

July 24, 1783	Born Simón José Antonio de la Santissima Trinidad de Bolívar y Palacios, in Caracas, Venezuela
1799	Goes to Spain to study
May 1802	Marries María Teresa de Toro, in Madrid
June 1802	Returns to Caracas
Jan. 1803	Bolívar's wife dies
1804	Bolívar returns to Europe
	Napoleon crowned emperor of France
1808	Napoleon conquers Spain and places his brother, Joseph, on the throne
July 5, 1811	Venezuela declares independence
April—July 1812	Bolívar conducts first military campaign
July 28, 1812	First Republic of Venezuela finally crushed when Spanish forces enter Caracas
Aug. 6, 1813	Bolívar, retured from exile in New Granada, recaptures Caracas and declares Second Republic of Venezuela
April 11, 1814	Napoleon abdicates and goes into exile
May 4, 1814	Ferdinand VII regains the Spanish throne and issues decree signalling return to despotism
June 15, 1814	Bolívar defeated at Battle of La Puerta, concedes fall of Second Republic of Venezuela, and flees to Cartagena
May 14, 1815	Bolívar arrives in Jamaica, attempts to gain British support
Dec. 6, 1815	Spanish forces enter Cartagena, regaining New Granada
1816	Bolívar returns to Venezuela with expeditionary force
Jan. 1819	Congress of Angostura instituted
Feb. 15, 1819	Bolívar elected president of the Third Republic of Venezuela
Aug. 7, 1819	Spanish forces defeated at Battle of Boyacá
Dec. 17, 1819	Venezuela and New Granada merge as Gran Colombia
June 24, 1821	Battle of Carabobo ends Spanish occupation of New Granada
June 29, 1821	Bolívar returns to Caracas and is declared president of Colombia
April 22, 1822	Quito (modern Ecuador) secured at Battle of Bomboná and incorporated into Gran Colombia
July 26, 1822	Bolívar meets San Martín at Guayaquil
Aug. 1824	Bolívar campaigns and gains victory at Battle of Junín
Dec. 9, 1824	Last Spanish army in South America defeated at Battle of Ayacucho Bolívar named president of High Peru
1826	Congress of Panama
Sept. 25, 1828	Attempted assassination of Bolívar in Bogotá
March 1830	Gran Colombia dissolves as Ecuador and Venezuela secede
May 8, 1830	Bolívar expelled from Venezuela
Dec. 17, 1830	Bolívar dies of tuberculosis in Santa Marta, Colombia

Further Reading

Beláunde, Victor. *Bolívar and the Political Thought of the Spanish-American Revolution.* Baltimore: Octagon Press, 1966.

Johnson, John J. *Simón Bolívar and Spanish-American Independence.* New York: Van Nostrand, 1968.

Lynch, John. *The Spanish-American Revolutions, 1808–1826.* New York: W.W. Norton, 1973.

Madariaga, Salvador de. *Simón Bolívar.* Coral Gables, Florida: University of Miami Press, 1952.

Masur, Gerhard. *Simón Bolívar.* Albuquerque, New Mexico: University of New Mexico Press, 1948.

Paine, Lauren. *Bolívar, the Liberator.* New York: Taplinger, 1970.

Prago, Albert. *The Revolution in South America: The Independence Movements of 1808–1825.* New York: Macmillan, 1970.

Trend, J.B. *Bolívar and the Independence of Latin America.* New York: Scholarly Press, 1948.

Worcester, Donald E. *Bolívar.* Boston: Houghton Mifflin, 1977.

Index

absolutism,   9, 34
Angostura *see* Ciudad Bolívar
Angostura, Congress of,   87–89, 91
Argentina,   44, 48, 72, 82, 95, 99, 101, 105
   see also San Martín, José de
Atahualpa,   61
Ayacucho, Battle of,   77, 92, 99, 102
   see also Sucre, Antonio José de
Beethoven, Ludwig van,   34, 35
Blakemore, Harold,   102
Bogotá,   69, 85, 91
   see also Colombia
Bolívar, Juan Vincente,   47, 60
Bolívar, Simón
   ancestry,   14
   attempted assassinations of,   85, 104
   Bolivia, president of,   101
   Boves, José Tomás, battle with,   80
   childhood,   17–25
   Ecuador, conquest of,   94
   European travels,   36-38
   exile,   105-107
   France, visit to,   28–36
   Greater Colombia
     creation of,   91
     president of,   91, 94, 99, 101–105
   Italy, stay in,   36–38
   Jamaica, stay in,   81–85
   London, visit to,   52
   Manifesto of Cartagena,   70, 71
   marriage,   29
   Miranda, Francisco, association with,
     51, 52, 59, 60, 62-64
   New Granada
     return to,   81
     stay in,   69
   Paris, stay in, 31
   San Martín, José de, meeting with,   95
   South American federation, dream of,
     102
   Spain
     journey to,   24–25, 27
     return to,   30–31
   underground activities,   47
   Venezuela
     constitution, formation of,   87–89
     government, role in,   50–53, 57,
       78–80, 89, 94
     march on,   71–75, 86

   return to,   43
Bolivia,   98, 101, 105
Bomboná, Battle of,   94
Bonaparte, Joseph,   13, 43, 44, 53
Botocudo Indians,   18
Bourbon, House of,   46
Boves, José Tomás,   75, 77, 79–81, 89
Boyacá, Battle of,   91, 97
Brazil,   18, 20, 104
Briggs,   H. P., 17
Britain *see* Great Britain
Buenos Aires, 82
    see also Argentina
Canning, George,   101, 102
Carabobo, Battle of,   94, 96
Caracas,   25, 46, 54, 59, 60, 63, 75, 79-81,
     94, 105 , 106
Carnevali, Atilano,   30
Cartagena, Colombia,   66, 69, 70, 85
Casa León, Marqués de,   47, 67
Catherine the Great,   41
Cervantes, Miguel de,   21, 23
Chacabuco, 72
    see also O'Higgins, Bernardo
Charles IV,   16, 27–29, 44
Chile,   48, 72, 80, 82, 83, 95
    see also O'Higgins, Bernardo; San Martín,
     José de
Churchill, Winston,   8
Ciudad Bolívar (Bolívar City, formerly
     Angostura),   86
Colombia,   48, 51, 66, 69, 105,
colonialism,   15, 18, 22, 62, 92, 104
Columbus, Christopher,   38
Common Sense,   49, 70
conquistadores,   17, 50, 61, 104
Contasini, Mario,   8
Coro,   42, 63
Cortez, Hernando,   38
creole,   14–17, 23, 30, 43, 45–46, 60, 67, 77,
    83
Danton, Georges,   19
de Tocqueville, Alexis,   9
de Toro, María Teresa,   27, 29
Declaration of Independence *see* United States
Declaration of the Rights of Man *see* France
Defoe, Daniel,   36, 37
democracy,   9, 10, 42, 59, 77, 88
Democracy in America,   9

Dessalines, Jean-Jacques, 86
Díaz, José, 61
divine right, 9, 60
Don Quixote, 18, 21, 23, 106
   see also Cervantes, Miguel de
du Villars, Fanny, 31
Ecuador, 48, 67, 69, 94, 103, 105
El Libertador see Bolívar, Simón
Emancipation Proclamation, 88
Emerson, Ralph Waldo, 10, 11
Emile, 22
   see also Rousseau, Jean-Jacques
Emparán, Vincente de, 47–49
England *see* Great Britain
equality, 20, 38
Eroica see Third Symphony
España, José María de, 23
Federalist Papers, 10
Ferdinand VII (Ferdinand of Asturias), 13,
     44–47, 50, 52, 53, 55, 56, 65, 71,
     82–84, 101
France, 15, 27–29, 33, 34, 38, 41, 47, 50,
     64, 78, 85–87, 94, 95
   Declaration of the Rights of Man, 38
   French Revolution, 19, 32
   Spain, involvement with, 13, 16, 43–45,
     56, 101
freedom, 7, 20, 38
Führerprinzip, 9
Godoy, Manuel de, 27, 29
Goya, Francisco, 28
Gran Colombia see Greater Colombia,
   Republic of
Great Britain, 41, 44, 45, 47, 49–52, 55, 64,
     66, 69, 84, 85, 96, 101, 102
Greater Colombia, Republic of, (*Gran
     Colombia*), 91, 94, 99, 101–105
Gual, Manuel, 23
Guatemala, 102
Guayaquil, 79, 95, 99
Haiti, 85–87, 94, 95
   see also Pétion, Alexandre
Hamilton, Alexander, 10
Hannibal, 90
Hidalgo y Costilla, Miguel, 73, 78
High Peru *see* Bolivia
Hipólita, 17, 18
History of the American People, 84
Hitler, Adolf, 8

Humboldt, Alexander von, 31, 32, 36
Incas, 93
Indians, 17, 18, 22, 23, 43, 49, 50, 61, 66,
     73, 75, 77, 78, 90, 93
Inquisition, 31, 51
Italy, *see* Bolívar, Simón
Iturbe, Francisco, 67
Iturbide, Agustín de, 102
   see also creole
Jamaica *see* Bolívar, Simón
Jamaica Letter, 84
James, William, 8
Josephine, 78
Junín, Battle of, 80, 93, 99
La Guaira, 60, 64
La Puerta, Battle of, 80
Larrazábal, Felipe, 60
Le Cap, 95
   see also Haiti
Lenin, 8
Letourneur, René, 67
Libertador see Bolívar, Simón
Life of the Liberator Simón Bolívar, 60
Lima, Peru, 19, 24, 61, 74, 98
Lincoln, Abraham, 10, 11, 88, 91
llaneros, 75, 77, 80, 89, 94
London *see* Bolívar, Simón
L'Ouverture, Toussaint, 86, 87
Lynch, John, 85
Machu Picchu, 93
Madison, James, 77
Madrid, 15, 65
Manifesto of Cartagena, 70, 71
Marengo, 37
María Luisa, 16, 27
Mariño, Santiago, 79, 80, 94
Mexico, 66, 73, 78, 102, 105
Miranda, Francisco, 41–43, 51–52, 59–60,
     62–67, 69
Mompox, 72
Monte Sacro, ("Sacred Mountain"), 37, 38
Monteverde, Juan Domingo, 60, 63–65, 67,
     74, 75, 83
Morillo, Pablo, 83, 85, 90, 93, 94
Morison, Samuel Eliot, 84
Napoleon, 13, 16, 27–29, 31, 33–35, 37,
     43–45, 48, 50, 64, 65, 78, 81, 82, 87
New Granada, 69, 70, 72, 75, 81, 85, 90, 91,
     97, 105

Niebuhr, Reinhold,   10
O'Higgins, Bernardo,   72, 80, 83
   see also Chacabuco; Chile
O'Leary, Daniel Florencio,   90
Organization of American States,   85, 102
Páez, José Antonio,   63, 89, 90, 94, 97, 101, 103
Paine, Thomas,   48, 49, 69, 70
Panama,   69, 85, 102
Pan-American Union,   102
Paris,   27, 31
Patagonia,   18
   see also Indians
Patriotic Society,   53
Pedro I,   104
   see also Brazil
Peru,   17, 19, 22, 24, 44, 61, 71, 74, 77, 79, 80, 82, 92, 93, 95, 97–99, 101–103, 105
   see also San Martín, José de
Pétion, Alexandre,   85, 86, 95
Piar, Manuel,   86
Pitt, William,   41, 49
Pizarro, Francisco,   61
Port Antonio,   84
Portugal,   104
Puerto Cabello,   63, 69, 75, 78–79
Ribas, José Felix, 80-81
Rights of Man, The,   49, 69
   see also Paine, Thomas
Robespierre, Maximilien,   32
Robinson Crusoe,   36, 37
Rochambeau, Jean Baptiste,   94
Rodríguez, Simón,   18, 20, 22–24, 28, 36–38, 43
Roman Catholic Church,   31, 51, 60–61
Rome,   37–39
Roosevelt, Franklin D.,   8
Rousseau, Jean-Jacques,   20, 22, 36, 37, 78
Russia,   41, 64
Sáenz, Manuela, 104
Saint-Domingue see Haiti

St. Helena,   81
Sámano, Juan,   85, 91
San Martín, José de,   24, 44, 71, 72, 79, 82, 95, 97, 99
   see also Argentina; Peru
Santa Marta, Colombia,   72
Santander, Francisco de Paula,   73, 79, 90–92, 94, 103, 104
slavery,   20, 30, 43, 49, 85–89, 91, 94, 95
Social Contract, The,   20
Spain,   13, 15–17, 24, 28, 29, 30, 44–48, 50–52, 55, 56, 59, 60, 63–67, 69–72, 74, 75, 77–82, 85, 86, 90–97, 99, 101, 102, 104
   Inquisition,   31
   Napoleon, intervention of,   43
   native South Americans, treatment of,   18, 50, 61
   South America, policies in,   14, 22, 23, 43, 53, 65, 83
   Venezuelan revolt, suppression of,   41, 42
Spanish American Revolutions,   85
Sucre, Antonio José de,   77, 92, 94, 99, 105
Talavera, Battle of,   47
Tenerife,   72
Third Symphony (Eroica),   34, 35
   see also Beethoven, Ludwig van
Tierra del Fuego,   18
Tolstoy, Leo,   7
United States,   9, 15, 38, 41, 42, 48–50, 59, 60, 76, 77, 86, 88, 91, 101–103, 105
   Declaration of Independence,   38
Urica, Battle of,   80, 81
Venezuela,   14, 22, 23, 32, 41–43, 47–52, 54, 57, 59, 60, 63–67, 69–75, 77–81, 83, 86–91, 94, 95, 103–107
   slavery,   30, 89, 91
Washington, George,   30, 76, 101
Wellington, Arthur Wellesley,   44
Wilson, Woodrow,   8
Zangara, Giuseppe,   8

Dennis Wepman has a graduate degree in linguistics from Columbia University and has written widely on sociology, linguistics, popular culture, and American folklore. He now teaches English at Queens College for the City University of New York. His special interest in Latin America has made him a lifetime student of its history and people.

Arthur M. Schlesinger, jr. taught history at Harvard for many years and is currently Albert Schweitzer Professor of the Humanities at City University of New York. He is the author of numerous highly praised works in American history and has twice been awarded the Pulitzer Prize. He served in the White House as special assistant to Presidents Kennedy and Johnson.

0/12 12/03 6-7-00-9